RISK LEADERSHIP

RISK LEADERSHIP

THE COURAGE TO CONFRONT & CHALLENGE

Curtis L. Brungardt, Ph.D.

C. B. Crawford, Ph.D.

a division of the *Rocky Mountain Institute for Leadership Advancement*
Longmont, Colorado

ROCKY MOUNTAIN PRESS
a division of the Rocky Mountain Institute for Leadership Advancement
524 Emery Street
Longmont, CO 80501
(303) 684-6480

ORDERING INFORMATION:
For individual sales, quantity sales, and orders for college textbook/course adoption use contact the publisher at the address listed above.

Cover Design: Amy Koehn
Typeset and Editing: Katherine A. Bollig
Editing Services: Liza Krug

Printed in the United States of America

Library of Congress Catalog Card Number: 99-90639

ISBN 1-929149-01-8

To my children Sara and Drake
– C.L.B.

To Janet, Dane, Andrea, & Alek,
who have given so much to me – C.B.C.

TABLE OF CONTENTS

PART II MANDATE TO CONFRONT AND CHALLENGE

PART III EMPLOYING THE REVOLUTIONARY MANDATE

PART IV RISK LEADERSHIP: THE MANDATE IS CLEAR

Preface

Risk Leadership was born out of a frustration with what we saw as a gap between the words and deeds of corporate leaders. Current literature, statements made by organizational leaders, and even our classroom lectures describe contemporary leadership approaches that promote and encourage *empowerment* and *organizational change*. However, in our extensive consulting work from the east coast to the midwest, we found a very different world. Employees from both public and private agencies told us endless stories about controlling managers who had little or no concern for real organizational change. While these managers preached empowerment and transformation, in reality, they were more interested in controlling the actions of subordinates and consolidating their own power. As a result we recognize and state openly, where others will not, that there is a tremendous gap between contemporary leadership and management theories and the actual practice of those models.

We have two primary purposes for writing this book: first, we want to expose the weaknesses of top managers and their approaches to leadership; and secondly, we want this book to be a call for all organizational players to assume more responsibility for leadership. We want upper management to actually think about what they are doing and how they are doing it. Many call themselves facilitators and collaborators, when in fact, they operate no differently from managers thirty years ago. While they pay lip-service to contemporary styles, most top managers focus more time and energy on issues that revolve around protecting their personal power arrangements and profits. Finally, this book is a call for employees at all levels to stand up and take responsibility for their organizations. We want to encourage low and mid-level workers to challenge status quo thinking, and more importantly, not to follow management blindly. It is the responsibility of each of us to lead the organizations in which we participate.

Although some may claim that we are not fair to modern empowerment practices, we on the other hand, have lost the faith. They may even state that some improvement has been made and more time is needed to fully implement these practices. We, however, are not patient enough to wait for these current leadership approaches. We admit that fault. You should not be patient either. While we understand that risk leadership is forward-looking and requires you to face challenges that you have never confronted before, we believe that the benefits are great enough to justify the risk. The way we see it, you can either wait thirty years for modern leadership efforts to give you real empowerment (maybe), or you can take command now and usher in this new and exciting era for leadership. Do you have the fortitude to be part of the organization of the future? We believe risk leadership will be one of the cornerstones of the future organization.

Risk Leadership: The Courage to Confront & Challenge takes a radical approach to leadership, change, and organizational improvement. We depart from the traditional and contemporary views of leadership in which the leaders or power figures serve as change agents for their organizations. Instead, we believe that most change agents are not recognized leaders or power figures, but rather are low and mid-level employees. Managers are often uniquely disempowered to effect change because the power structures reassert stability and suppress change when risk is felt. Top managers, as well as low and mid-level employees, need to recognize the weaknesses of contemporary change models that are primarily top-down and reinforce status quo, quick-fix solutions. This model encourages low and mid-level employees to confront and challenge status quo authority for the purpose of transforming their organizations. Furthermore, this theory seeks to establish a corporate culture that not only accepts, but also expects, confrontation and challenge to enhance problem solving, decision making, and overall organizational performance. Finally, this book challenges lower level employees to "step up to the plate" and not wait for the power structure to transform their corporation.

Curtis L. Brungardt
C. B. Crawford
May, 1999

Acknowledgements

This book would be little more than a shell without the insights we gained from talking with thousands of people over the last decade in our organizational work. Their perspectives have given us the impetus to write a theory that is both controversial, yet necessary. We especially thank many of those in authority positions who have shown great management, but poor leadership at times.

Our theory would lack maturity if it were not for the help of some key Fort Hays State University faculty that provided encouragement, ideas, and editing. In addition, our classrooms have served as experimental labs for testing and critiquing this theory. Our undergraduate and graduate students have been receptive to this new approach and have become both honest critics and advocates.

Finally, we gratefully acknowledge those pioneers that have stepped forward as risk leaders. They serve as role models for all of us. Their successes provide encouragement and motivation for those aspiring to confront and challenge the status quo.

TRANSITION IN LEADERSHIP

This introductory section discusses the evolution of leadership thinking from classical or traditional models to the more contemporary progressive approaches. The flaws of these earlier theories are discussed and a new model called risk leadership is proposed.

Chapter 1

Classical Leadership: The Will to Stabilize and Control

Introduction

Leadership has been an important issue for centuries. From the era of Roman Caesars and the days of Attila the Hun, the effectiveness of leadership was often measured in blood. In medieval times, dark robes and the grave fear of the absolute authority of one man provided leadership over others. In the Napoleonic battles, as well as our own Revolutionary war, this concern became more noble, but no less ruthless. In each millennia, people have been concerned with the military, political, and spiritual leaders of their particular eras. Many great thinkers have examined the role of effective and ineffective leaders from the battlefield to the temple. The leaders carrying the biggest "stick," measured by the heartiest troops and the most modern weaponry, were considered the leaders of men.

With the introduction of industrialized techniques, the popular study of leadership became much more centered on the modern organization. Many scholars and great thinkers claimed that effective leaders spur maximum production. The role of the worker, while not as disposable as in barbaric eras, was certainly that of a servant. Leaders in the industrial era were generally wasteful of the valuable human resources that kept them in power. Leadership was measured not by body counts as before, but by the number of rifles produced, bricks laid, or bushels of cotton picked. The results of this era, although literally different from the barbaric centuries, were figuratively similar to the extent that humans were considered a means to an end.

As the industrialized world moves into the era of information and knowledge, the role of the leader is no less important. As we approach the year 2000, leaders face many of same challenges of their predecessors in the year 1 AD. People still fight over dirt. The political arena still has many corrupt and deceitful elements. And the workplace is much like a battlefield or factory floor where work is compulsory, despite the concerns of important constituents - the workers.

This chapter describes the classical leader in the most general sense. Although many scholars believe that classical leadership suffered the same fate as prehistoric dinosaurs, current evidence suggests that many classical leaders still walk the factory floors and office halls. While some may look at the means classical leaders used as antique, they often did and do produce the necessary results. However, the cost of that production was and still is beared by many unskilled and "disposable" workers. This chapter explores the characteristics and assumptions made about classical leadership.

Assumptions of Classical Leadership

Classical leaders have several guiding convictions which pattern their leadership style. The assumptions of classical leadership have remained consistent since before the dark ages. For many classical leaders, their purpose and methods can be simplified by two very primitive principles: the will to stabilize and the will to control. In classical leadership, leading is simply the use of power and position to achieve the maximum production possible in a manner that promotes stability and control. The following assumptions about classical leadership revolve around these two themes.

The first assumption is that "leaders have the 'right' and even the 'duty' to lead." As the key element of the workplace, leaders are often given a great deal of authority over day-to-day functioning of staff members and other employees. This is not news. Everyone knows that leaders have the authority to make decisions, confront issues, hold others accountable, hire and evaluate employees on a daily basis. For classical leaders, this responsibility takes the form of a duty, or right, to perform leadership in the way they see best. This right or duty, handed down by members of the next level of management, the CEO, or even from divine sources, is unquestionable in any form. As children, we too faced and reluctantly accepted the classical argument: "do it because I said so," from our parents.

In less civilized times, the "right" to lead often came through two complimentary forms. First, the right to lead came from a legacy like a kingdom, or the confirmation of spiritual purity. The second form, fear, often followed the first and was usually even more compelling. Because people understood the divine right of a few to rule the many, there was fear of the consequences that these few could muster against the masses. Everyone understood the atrocious behavior of a few members of the nobility and the church. These acts of power stood as a strong deterrent to possible change agents that stood watching in the crowd as people died for their insurrection.

This form of leadership worked because the contribution of subordinates was limited to taking orders and following directions. Classical leaders generally share the belief that workers are inefficient, and if left to their own devices, would not perform at a satisfactory level. Leaders under this model generally use more direct, and sometimes coercive, means to get the job done.

The second assumption is that "not everyone can lead." Leadership is not for everyone. Classical leaders embrace the notion that leadership is special. Like the Holy Grail of an organization (the company policy manual), there is a definite mystic quality surrounding leadership. This special quality eludes the mortal worker since they can not fully understand and appreciate the complexities of leadership. Leadership, to the classicist, is held at the top, by the few, for the few, and with the best interests of themselves and the company in mind. These goals have little latitude for concern of the worker, and maximize the power of the few...the suits. To the classical leader, the world is black and white. The shades of gray are just anomalies and are dealt with through policy and the unyielding decision-making process. In the world of the classical leader, the only people with leadership duties are leaders. Their position gives them further justification to lead.

The third assumption is that "leaders can do as they wish as long as they get results." Knowing the "why" and "what" of classical status quo leadership is one thing, but knowing the "how" is quite another. While the effects and results emerging from classical leadership are quite direct and astounding, the methods that are used to achieve these results range from obvious "power plays" to covert "sting operations." One of the best known notions pertaining to classical management is that managers do what it takes to get the job done in the most expedient and efficient manner possible.

It takes little imagination to think of examples where the ends justified the means. Perhaps a most striking example comes from the traditional drill sergeant and the basic training recruit. The drill sergeant is given the difficult task of leading new recruits to an outcome that is so foreign to them that often "shock management" must be performed. To make tough soldiers out of new recruits, a kinder and gentler drill sergeant approach will not work. Instead, as has been done for centuries, recruits are subjected to more than strenuous exercise, sleep and hygiene deprivation, extreme hunger and thirst, mental and often physical abuse. Of course people excuse this behavior since it has always been done this way and it seems to work. Still, for many recruits this approach borders inhumane.

The fourth assumption is that "labor must be divided." Classical leaders will often divide the labor for the purposes of efficiency, maintaining control, and supporting allies. By creating specialized divisions and developing interdependent workflow processes, large and complex organizations can produce consistent and efficient outcomes. In addition, by dispersing the workforce, management is better equipped to control and squander internal dissention. Finally, the division of labor is a tool which the leader utilizes to promote those in favor by exposing only them to the jobs that lead to promotion, while withholding those same jobs from people in less favor.

In traditional sweatshop labor situations this was perhaps the most visible function of leadership. If you were in poor favor with the management of the time, your hours (and hence your lifestyle) would suffer. If, however, you were in favor with management you would be allowed to work long hours, doing back-breaking work, for a mere pittance. Thus, these workers would go home satisfied with the abuses they endured.

The fifth assumption is that "leaders create policies that organize and control." This is done in a variety of ways. Policies (rules, company handbooks, unspoken laws, etc.) serve the purpose of keeping leaders in power and keeping workers working. Policies serve to stabilize, organize, and make efficient the roughly inefficient worker in a chaotic organization. Policies keep the status quo working, and keep change to a minimum. Large and historic corporate giants like *General Motors* and *IBM* utilize policies in order to serve the leader's wishes. We all know that most policies are infinitely regressive; you can always build more policies for the policies that you have just codified. For example, empowerment is an acceptable strategy in the workplace to the extent that the policy manual allows it. Then, only by following the stringent 5-step approach of the policy writer and the approval committee, can the strategy actually be implemented.

In their purest sense, the role of policies is often to substitute for creative managerial solutions in the face of unique situations. The "unique situation" is exactly what policy manuals attempt to defy. To say that invoking policy has been a driving force for the success of organizations would only be partially true! The fact of the matter is that policies, and the rituals that are associated with those policies, are just easy ways of getting out of doing the real work that leaders should be doing...leading!

The sixth assumption is that "leaders must invoke fear to control the masses." In other organizations there may be fewer rules; therefore, classical leaders turn to more direct methods to stabilize and control. The only thing that can create compliance quicker than a policy is the fear of a classical leader's wrath. Though informal, this type of control can be just as motivating as any formal policy. This informal policy builds a wall of control around the leader's kingdom. This wall becomes most problematic when followers, out of fear and excessive control, actually prop up the leader and allow status quo thinking to rule. Change agents cannot permeate this wall. Fear and control have now squashed all hopes of changing the very system that allows the leader the authority they need to strike fear.

One type of behavior which instills fear is that of the "random bullet" leader. If a leader lashes out in response to a situation, and does not in another, this sends a clear message that the leader is not consistent with the very punishment they use to control. Often times, this form of behavior exerts the most control since it creates constant fear in workers. Behaviors that were once acceptable can suddenly become offensive. Workers' stature with the leader can change based on the "mood of the day". This type of classical leader, though seemingly more reasonable at first glance, is nothing more than a spoiled brat with a badge.

The seventh assumption is that "leaders view workers as incompetent and lazy." According to classical leaders, most workers lack the necessary skills and would not function productively without their direct supervision. Typically, these classicists believe that the average employee lacks self-motivation and initiative. Realistically, workers have no real incentive to do their jobs since classical leadership regulates and restricts any individuality, growth, or fun in the workplace. Simply, these gratuities are not needed in order to meet the bottom line. People come to work to work, not to have fun, after all. If people want to enjoy themselves they can do it after work. The workplace is not the right place to enjoy oneself, as we all know.

So workers go to their jobs, day after day and do the same dull and unempowering job over and over. Laziness becomes programmed into the workplace to the extent that people have no control over improvements of the system or their workplace. Suggestion boxes often go unused by all organizational parties. Whistle blowing is a sacrilege even if there is criminal action or obvious incompetence involved. Furthermore, workers are lulled into a sense of security and stability, even if the stability is not very appealing. Workers have blind faith in management, given the stability of this system. This blind faith becomes the hood over the face of social change right before the axe of stability and status quo thinking falls.

The eighth assumption is that "classical leaders follow the Golden Rule of Management - those with the most gold, rule!" This thinking creates a degree of exclusiveness within the ranks of leadership, since not everyone can be a player when the classical leader throws funding at those areas that best meet their objectives. Leaders promote those within "the club" and those outside the box are minimalized, trivialized, and tokenized if need be. Classical leadership does not reward diversity, cultural or pragmatic, unless forced to or if the diversity becomes co-opted and mainstreamed. After all, if the classical leader holds all the rewards, then the organization should bend to their desires, rather than the needs of other less fortunate worker types.

The ninth assumption is that "leaders must be decisive to be productive." Since decision making is where money is made or lost, classical leaders must be quick and emotionally detached in their decision making. Classical leaders don't pass on making decisions, since this would illustrate both weakness and a lack of control. As a result, they make decisions that could easily be made by those below them with more information. Subordinate workers exist to work, not to make the decisions about work.

Classical leaders are detached, unemotional, efficient, and mechanical. Classical leadership thinking says that leaders, at their best, should be resolute in their determination to depersonalize the job of decision making and leading others. Leaders keep others at a distance to ensure that personal attachment will not "cloud their good judgment." The mechanical nature of leading others is reinforced by the fact that leaders follow policy to make decisions, rather than making decisions based upon employee concerns.

In retrospect, the purpose and methods of classical leadership are decisive, commanding, controlling, and unquestionable. Leaders are right since no one has the power to question or defy orders. The most effective leaders are those that can impose structure on chaotic organizations. The capacity to organize cannot be emphasized enough for the classical leader. Given the fact that the classicist desires stability and minimal change, formal structure is the ultimate way of codifying what is good in the organization. Consequently, the bad parts are structured as far away as possible from the leadership. When you look at any number of organizational charts prior to the 1960s, you will quickly notice that there were often 4, 5, or even as many as 6 levels of management between the CEO and the line worker. Management created a linking system where one person had a span of authority over their subordinates. Leaders above that person had a span of control that extended to others. This thinking led organizations to become departmentalized as opposed to being unified.

Results from Classical Leadership

Of all things that could be said about classical leadership, the ability to generate results must be near the top of the list of truisms. Classical leaders are able to generate productivity in a most direct manner. Through fear, command, control, and manipulation, classical leaders are able to push production to the efficient limit, and maintain that level as long as the leader maintains control and stability. Unfortunately, that control often fades due to burnout, excessive attrition, or organizational transfers, all of which make efficient production more elusive than the stability the classical leader desires. Two distinct results have emerged from the vast history of classical leadership. This particular style has produced: efficiency and stability, as well as a division between the haves and havenots.

First, classical leadership has been the poster child for efficiency and consistent production. Historically, classical leaders have been able to produce, when other methods have failed. To see the results of classical leadership, you only need to look as far as wartime industries in Europe and the United States. While much of the factory work was led by dictatorial and autocratic practices, the resulting production was massive enough to win wars. The modern educational industry has also been patterned on this template. Students have been herded through the system in the most efficient method possible. These tendencies have been institutionalized not just in policy, but also in the content students are taught. For example, accounting and management principle classes have become the mainstream tools for teaching people about leadership.

The basic result of this efficiency mindset has been more comprehensive than perhaps we even know. Efficiency has invaded our being. The arts, possibly the last bastion for the fight against stability, have become mass-produced at every possible chance. Businesses are evaluated on the basis of the balance sheet as opposed to the employee's needs, the values they enact, or the greater good they produce for the community and the world around them. Efficiency has given the leader an objective basis for judging either good and bad, or right or wrong. These practices in many ways have eliminated the gray area for personal judgement in decision making. The essence of this push has been a depersonalization of the workplace, perhaps even dehumanization.

Another outcome of this efficiency has been the proliferation of organizational stability. Change is seen as disruptive to the workflow and allows more error and chance in the business equation. Profit is critical to the organization as well; every day without profit is failure. A threat to stability is seen as a threat to profits. Business models are predicated on this very assumption. Stability in the past has provided the modern organization with consistency and predictability in both productivity and profitability. In addition, this stable condition has created a comfortable environment for all organizational players.

This focus on stability has also provided the foundation for the development of the modern bureaucracy. This allows classical leaders to hide behind rules, regulations, and polices. The bureaucracy allows leaders to build power in uncontrolled ways in order to protect and benefit themselves, while exploiting others (even the company in some cases). Bureaucracy, or the unfettered practice of building department and policy upon department and policy, is considered the popular model of efficiency. The bureaucratic structure focuses on self-reservation and stability, as well as the death of both individuality and spontaneous organizational change. This approach takes the perspective that the organization should not depend on any one person. Even classical leaders can be replaced by other more stable and efficient classical leaders.

Second, division between the haves and the havenots has become endemic in the classical leadership model. Classical leaders reward those who are willing subjects of their version of leadership. The division becomes more institutionalized when leaders promote ONLY those who act like they do, lead like they do, or look like they do. Even though bureaucracies have adopted policies that promote traditionally divided entities, the classical leader finds ways of using those policies that serve their ends and finding other policies to subvert the integration. Not to mislead, a division that has concerned a great number of people in the last 20 or 30 years is the division based on civil rights of minority groups. However, the divisions to which we refer here are not limited to minority divisions, but rather are based on socio-economic factors (where your kids go to school, the color of your hair, whether or not you have facial hair), and other points of personal issue for a classical leader. Division becomes a way of life for the classicist. Promotions based on efficiency may take a back seat to arbitrary divisions because the absolute power of the classicist gives them the to do as they wish with no questions asked.

Summary

Classical leadership is really more about leaders, not leadership or followers. Classicists use methods that are focused on their personal gain or organizational objectives rather than the needs of the greater collective. The real method of classical leadership is top-down rather than peer, collaborative, or bottom-up. Classical leadership offered the peace and stability that was necessary for an uneducated and unmotivated workforce. In the industrial era, the efficiency of classical leadership was essential in order to maximize the benefits and minimize costs. Classical leadership was expected and somewhat appropriate given the circumstances of that era.

Classical leadership, though important for centuries, is not responsive enough for success in the current fast-paced business environment. Classical leadership, with its bloated bureaucracy and drive for stability, dooms the modern organization to mediocrity. Modern organizations, recognizing this trend in the 1970s and 1980s, embarked on a new method to lead others - the *progressive leadership* approach. The basic question that many people started asking was "do the ends of stability and productivity justify the means of autocratic and inconsistent use of power?" The answer by many was a resounding "NO!" Progressive leadership is many things that classical leadership is not. Progressive leadership is centered on change; classical leadership is focused on status quo. Progressive leadership is focused on responsive workers; classical leadership is focused on subservience. Progressive leadership offers many changes to the traditional command and control, autocratic mentality that classical leadership offers.

In today's "grow or die" mentality, we believe that stability is and will not be the ticket to organizational riches. Stability was the date we brought to the dance, but we better be thinking about other friends to leave with. As a method of leadership, the classical approach is severely flawed given it's top-down, autocratic nature. Still, many people around the world, and around your block, work in organizations that have not yet eliminated this form of activity. In fact, many organizational structures still promote this facade of success, results, and efficiency to the detriment of all of their employees. Classical leadership is alive and well in industrial America. The promise of progressive methods, however, is appearing as the grim reaper for many classical managers as the pool of leaders becomes more contemporary and demands new methods.

Chapter 2

Progressive Leadership: The Will to Change and Empower

Introduction

By the mid-1970s, it became apparent to most of corporate America that stability was no longer the prescription for organizational health. Relatively easy growth that had served the 1950's, 1960's and much of the 1970s was no longer holding true. Business leaders throughout America realized that economic conditions were much more competitive and volatile. The corporate environment was experiencing tremendous changes. A combination of increased market and global competition, regulatory demands, new microeconomic trends, technological changes, and demographical shifts in the workplace all led to this new business climate. Simply put, status quo thinking and slow incremental organizational change and improvement would no longer be enough for survival. Thus, the will to stabilize was not going to be the answer for organizational success, but rather, a ticket to sure failure.

Purposes of Progressive Leadership

Business leaders began to realize that they would have to increase quality and reduce costs to insure growth, compete, and survive in this new environment. Transformational change and progressive leadership would need to replace the incremental approaches of classical leadership. Therefore, corporate leaders began playing a new game - *the change game*. In the 1980s and 1990s we experienced an explosion of new management techniques and approaches in order to enhance organizational growth. The quality movement (TQM, CQI, etc.), re-engineering methods, strategic thinking and planning, change management, organizational improvement, and transformational leadership were all attempts to implement major "change" in our companies. In the name of organizational success, managers and consultants alike were encouraging intervention strategies that truly altered the organization. The motto chanted by many was (and for that matter still is) – change or die! The will to stabilize no longer guaranteed growth, success, or even survival. The will to change had become the answer.

Over the last two decades or so, management consultants and scholars have introduced us to a wide-array of "change models and strategies." These vary from simple 1-2-3 management techniques and strategies for implementing change to very large, comprehensive, and elaborate models that are intended to transform the entire company. For example, one popular book on change talks about the need to follow a tight transition plan which includes describing the future state, identifying preconditions, evaluating abilities, developing a change master plan, and then communicating that change activity. Another book illustrates a model with conflicting forces. Here an innovation cycle interacts with the inevitable resistance cycle to produce movement. And yet another describes a three-part drama including the recognition for change, the creation of a vision, and strategies for institutionalizing the change. Although the literature makes organizational change sound like an easy step-by-step process that eventually leads to growth and success, the fact is the journey is never that simple. Those who have participated in serious transformation describe the process as a confusing endeavor filled with numerous wrong turns, missed opportunities, and varying amounts of both successes and failures.

In the process of writing this book, we studied numerous change models and interviewed dozens of managers who had survived (and some that had not) *the change game*. What we found was that every successful implementation of change goes through four basic phases. While these steps are easy to understand, they are anything but easy to carry out. First, the organization has to reach the point where it "refuses to accept things the way they are." For example, management refuses to accept the status quo. "What we are doing, how we are doing it, and the results of what we are doing are not acceptable anymore. We will not survive holding only one-tenth of the market share. We recognize and do not accept the fact that the quality of our product is less than our competitors." Very simply, if you never reach the point of unacceptability, you will never engage in transforming change.

In the second phase, the organization creates a vision for future success. Although we found this is usually developed by top management, any level of an organization can add value to the vision. The strategic vision provides the company with a road map and direction for the change. If change is about moving the organization from *what is* to *what ought to be*, then the mental vision is the creation of *what ought to be*. This could be as simple as a professional football team's goal of winning the NFL championship or a university seeking to double its enrollment.

In the third phase, those who serve as the change sponsors and agents (usually top management) must both initiate and communicate the vision and resulting change plan within the organization. Change agents must not only talk about the vision and create the detailed action steps for change; they need to make the initial movement that starts the process. In addition, these agents of change must be successful in communicating the vision, the detailed steps towards that goal, the obstacles to be overcome, and most importantly the purpose of the transformation. Their success will determine the level of commitment, compliance, and resistance they will encounter. In most firms, this usually takes place in company-wide forums or numerous staff meetings. Leadership lays out the vision and plan, listens to the rank and file, and then seeks commitment (or at the very least, compliance) from change recipients. Next, managers and line staff at all levels begin the process of implementing the change plan.

Finally, for the change to be successful, the entire organization (or at least most of it) must sustain the change. This is by far the most difficult part of the entire change process. After the initial excitement and enthusiasm is gone, once visual support from top management seems lacking, the troops are asked to carry on. This is the phase where most, if not all, failed change efforts stumble. Day in and day out managers and staff face an endless line of obstacles. Then the organization tires, and internal resistance gains momentum. Often, the change agents and change recipients look for the easier and simpler life

- going back to what we were doing before. Those organizations that can keep their focus and energy on reaching their vision through this difficult sustaining movement phase will more likely be successful in transformation.

As we have discussed earlier, the role of leadership for most of this century has been to stabilize the complex arrangements that make up the organization. However, today most recognize that this status quo management approach is not sufficient for today's dynamic and changing business climate. The task now facing business leaders is finding the best way to promote, encourage, and master the art of organizational change. In this new business climate, top management is now serving as "change agents," with the hope of transforming their organizations. Therefore, in the new environment, *the change game*, the leader's role has been transformed from an agent of stability to an agent of change. Their responsibility is now to provide the foresight and energy to carry change forward. This new and progressive leadership calls for leaders to move from their traditional roles and lead the organization through the painful process of real change.

As change agents, leaders serve as the visionaries. They create the vision and direction for the group. They clearly state what needs to change. In addition to providing this direction, they are the initiators of the change process. This includes both implementing and monitoring the change process. As progressive leaders they are responsible for directing the structure, processes, and the culture of the organization through the four phases of the change process.

Today's organizations look much different from the ones our parents served. The *change game* drives much of the thinking as well as the action. If the firm is going to survive, grow, and succeed, then transformation is the answer. At the same time, the role of management has changed to fit this new climate. Leaders are now change agents leading their employees through the difficult process of handling the resistance and obstacles they face when playing the *change game*.

Methods of Progressive Leaders

In addition to the overall purpose of leadership changing from status quo thinking to organizational change, so to has the method in which leaders pursue that change. The popular literature of today describes a completely different management style or approach. Instead of the traditional idea of leadership discussed in Chapter 1, in which a leader is tough-minded, in-control, and functions in a top-down situation, we now recognize that a leader needs to be a collaborator and facilitator in this volatile climate.

Business consultants, scholars, and many top mangers often talk about a world in which the traditional hierarchical organization doesn't work anymore. They tell us that the conventional command and control style of leadership (with power residing in higher positions) no longer produces the results needed in today's changing and competitive environment. Both scholars and practitioners alike describe in great detail the decline of the hierarchy. As a result, they encourage organizations to create new flexible structures and cultures that maximize the contributions of all employees.

Vietnam, Watergate, and numerous political scandals in the last several decades have also shown each of us not to follow our political leaders blindly. This same skepticism and attitude has carried over to the workplace. The result is that Baby Boomers and Generation-X employees are less impressed with authority. Simply, most of us are not willing to be led or managed in the traditional control style. More and more employees at all levels want to feel empowered and have more decision-making power in their work environment. Finally, experts also point to the availability of information as another reason to challenge the hierarchical structure. We now communicate more and with more people, and thus, are more knowledgeable about the organization.

Although there are many different types, styles, models, and approaches to empowerment, to some degree they all revolve around the simple concept of shared power. These models call for top management to transfer power to lower levels of the organization in the hopes of "maximizing the full potential" of all employees. Replacing the traditional top-down hierarchical structure, the new empowerment approach is described as a flat and flexible organization with informal collaborative and communication networks, decentralized accountability, and shared power. The purpose of this leadership style is to make the organization stronger by encouraging critical thinking and decision making by more and more employees. To be successful in today's business environment, all employees must contribute. Empowerment advocates tell us that the benefits are endless. By sharing power with everyone in the organization, we are in fact "unlocking the potential" of all employees.

Results from Progressive Leadership

The results of progressive leadership have been mixed at best. In the research for this book, we found several cases in which the leader *did* adequately play the role of a "collaborative change agent." They joined in partnership with their employees and successfully pursued transformational change. *Motorola*, *Harley-Davidson*, and the *Saturn* project are just a few limited examples of the success of progressive leadership. In these situations, management and staff worked side by side in more of a shared power environment in accomplishing real change. Although these cases illustrate the rewards of the progressive leadership model, we believe these examples are the exception rather than the rule. We do not deny that there have been limited successes of the organizational change and empowerment models; however, in most situations the results have been less impressive (a lot less impressive) than most would admit.

In our interviews with management and staff, we heard hundreds of stories about failed change efforts and so-called empowerment strategies that never really shared power. What we found was small and incremental change, and at best limited empowerment. Status quo thinking and top-down control still dominate the organizational landscape. While management often talked about the contemporary themes of change and empowerment, in the end most leaders were unwilling to relinquish control and power.

In theory, the concepts of organizational change and empowerment provide corporate America with useful models and ideas for sustaining growth. However, in reality these concepts have not been widely used. Rather, we find that most organizations today are experiencing incremental change and some top-down empowerment. In most cases, corporate leaders are tightly controlling the change process and strictly administering limited top-down empowerment strategies. With only limited use of the progressive leadership approach, management has threatened the very survival of the organization.

Although partial blame for the failure of progressive leadership must be carried by each of us, clearly it is top management who has not been willing to make the sacrifices needed to fully implement real change and empowerment. Honestly, most top managers are less than interested in true transformation. The current status quo situation benefits their control and power arrangement. By leaving their comfort zone and pursuing change, they threaten their future power base within the organization. When travelling down the path of change, there are no guarantees. In his book, *Deep Change*, Robert Quinn describes participation in the change process as "walking naked into a land of uncertainty." It is inevitable that in the change process, leaders (like the rest of us), lose more control over our environment. Thus, most managers are not willing to make this leap from incrementalism to transformationalism.

Current wisdom says, "empowerment starts at the top." Ultimately, it is top management who transfers power to the rank and file. The essence of this transfer rests with the leader's belief that his or her employees can use this power for the benefit of the organization. The problem, however, is that many companies nurture a leadership style and culture that reinforces the traditional hierarchical organization. While many managers talk about their empowering strategies, few are willing to test the shared power waters. In some cases command and control structures prohibit such action. Even beyond the bureaucracy, most leaders don't have the confidence or the willingness to surrender power to others. In our consulting work, we often found managers who were threatened by the entire concept of shared power. Simply, they feared a loss of power and control. The bottom line is that top-down empowerment remains only a concept.

Summary

Over the last two decades, much of the popular and academic literature on leadership and organizational improvement has focused on the progressive themes of change and empowerment. The primary purpose of leaders and the leadership process has been to implement and sustain transformational change. The will to change replaced the will to stabilize. This literature proclaimed that only through organizational transformation could one be successful in this competitive marketplace.

Concurrently, the methods of how leaders and managers lead has also changed. Progressive leaders serve more as collaborators or facilitators in today's business climate. Progressive leadership calls for a more horizontal organization with shared power structures. In addition, societal factors also put pressure on managers to alter their traditional leadership styles.

In the end, however, the progressive leadership approach has not produced the results desired by many. Although some successes can be recorded, very little transformational change and real empowerment has occurred. To date, many top managers do not show a willingness to alter the organizational landscape.

Chapter 3

Risk Leadership: The Will to Confront and Challenge

Introduction

If stability and control are not the answer for the 21st century organization - then what is? If change and empowerment are only theories that in today's environment have not truly been implemented - then what should we do? What future arrangements can be made to ensure, or at least encourage, organizational growth? With *risk leadership*, we break away from the classical and progressive approaches and propose a radically different model of leadership, change, and organizational improvement. Risk leadership will ask you to create a completely new mindset about your organization. It will ask you to make the leap from top-down management thinking to a bottom-up confrontational approach. Finally, it will ask you to take a different look at organizational power in general, and more importantly, the leader-follower empowerment arrangement.

Risk leadership departs from the traditional and contemporary views of leadership in which the leaders (power figures) serve as the uncontested change agents of their organizations. Instead, most true change agents are not the recognized leaders, but rather, are the lower-level energetic employees of the organization. Current power arrangements and supporting structures reassert stability and suppress change when challenge is felt by the leadership. It is important that top management, as well as low and mid-level employees, begin to recognize the weaknesses of contemporary change models.

The risk leadership model encourages low and mid-level employees to confront and challenge status quo authority for the purpose of transforming the organization. Furthermore, this model seeks to establish a corporate culture that not only accepts, but expects, confrontation and challenge as a way to enhance organizational performance. Finally, risk leadership calls on low and mid-level employees to assume responsibility and not wait for the traditional power structure to transform the corporation.

Failure of Classical and Progressive Leadership

Clearly, the traditional and contemporary approaches to leading organizations have not provided the successful growth many will need to survive. While some may say that things are just fine, what they are really describing slow death, or what John Gardner calls "a creeping crisis." Stability (or even incremental change) in today's volatile marketplace will no longer provide the company with the direction, the means, and more importantly, the right attitude to succeed.

Additionally, leading by a strong hierarchical command and control style in our current workplace will surely meet with the same unfavorable results. Although there are times in every organization where some short-term issues require strong leadership, over a protracted period of time, the 21st century employee will likely not be motivated to provide the resources needed. Simply, today's employees demand to participate in a much more democratic or shared power climate.

Similar to the classical approach, progressive leadership in most cases has failed to produce the organizational performance promised. However, contrary to the classical leadership style, the core principles of change and empowerment of progressive leadership do hold tremendous potential. As mentioned in Chapter 2, we believe management has never given the progressive model a chance. The lack of control over the situation and the reduction of power to make and implement decisions have forced many top managers to pursue safer approaches. Issues such as personal insecurities and power-driven egos have prohibited most from truly experimenting with transformational change and empowerment. Thus, the central flaw in the progressive leadership model is that it operates from a top-down mentality that is never overcome. It makes the assumption that top managers will have both the vision and the *courage* to transform their organizations in a shared power climate.

We believe the progressive leadership approach of transformational change and empowerment does in fact hold the appropriate keys to achieve organizational success. Our fundamental assumption is that those who hold the traditionally high hierarchical positions are not willing to make the personal sacrifices needed. When pressure is felt, most top managers are not willing to risk their own power arrangements to implement progressive leadership. While they may pay lip service to the concept, or even test it under "controlled conditions," in most cases they are not willing to fully endorse the approach. If top-down driven change and empowerment has not succeeded - then what is the answer? Clearly, a new model or approach is needed to implement transformational change and empowerment.

Why Confront and Challenge?

Why should you and I confront and challenge authority? Why should we initiate confrontation at the cost of personal risk? If our organizations are going to get better, even a little better, it will take much more than the decision making of top management. The growth of the organization, and even its survival, is too important to be left in the hands of the CEO and his or her lieutenants. If transformational change is to happen, then it is clearly up to the rank and file. If management will not share power, then it is up to the troops to seize power for the collective good of the organization. Therefore, the responsibility for the success or failure of the company not only rests with its leadership, but more importantly, with low and mid-level staffers who must challenge those traditional structures. Organizational health to a great extent, will be measured by the success of energetic and innovative employees who serve as *risk agents* that confront and challenge the ideas and the methods of the traditional change agents, top management.

The motivating factors that encourage these lower level workers, the risk agents, to participate in leading the company revolve around three pressure points - issues, people, and transformation. First, risk agents often mobilize around key issues of the time. They are issues that risk agents feel management has simply failed to address. This may include a missed opportunity or a problem area that management has not adequately solved. A lack of resources for the sales department, the need for modern equipment on the factory floor, or to counter a competitor's advantage could all be examples that may encourage an issue-driven revolt.

Secondly, the lack of effective leadership from top management could also lead to an internal revolt. This could include repeated errors of judgment and decision making, inappropriate behavior, or the abuse of power. What motivates the risk agents is their desire to defuse, replace, and correct the activities of the leadership. These employees recognize the weaknesses of their leaders and mobilize for the purposes of keeping the company on track.

Finally, the third explanation for why low and mid-level workers challenge authority rests with the simple idea that they are unhappy with the general performance of the organization. Risk agents believe their organization could be more, should be more, and that they can make it more. While this transformation-driven revolt usually includes concerns over particular issues and the lack of adequate leadership, it is much more broad-based and comprehensive. Risk agents believe that they are part of an "average" company. The organization is not meeting the needs and expectations of both employees and consumers. In this type of revolt, risk agents attempt to challenge management for the purpose of providing direction and leading the transformation.

Risk Agents and the Risk Agency

Risk agents are those who are not satisfied with the performance of the organization. They are low and mid-level employees who not only have a deep interest in their own careers, but also the performance of the organization as a whole. They are typically younger and newer to the company and are usually upwardly mobile. Risk agents are those in the organization who are viewed as energetic, enthusiastic, innovative, and most importantly, having a reputation for hard work and high performance. It is these very qualities that give them the organizational power to risk and challenge authority.

To successfully confront the organizational power structure, a single risk agent can not act alone. For that matter, two or three of the brightest employees will not survive in a long-term struggle against management. What is needed is an entire "coalition of revolutionaries" who empower themselves to challenge and transform the organization. This coalition is called a *risk agency* and operates on the premise, "the power of many." The formation of the risk agency provides the organizational structure with a new power entity. With a strong coalition, the risk agents have their best opportunity for success.

This informal cluster of revolutionaries shares many common beliefs. First, they have a strong belief that the company should and could be better. They see mediocrity all around them and are frustrated with what they see as little or no hope for improvement. Second, risk agents have lost faith in management's ability to successfully lead the organization. To them, top managers have little concern for the real issues of transformation and lack the courage to make difficult decisions.

Third, these risk agents believe they can play an active role in directing the future of the organization. To them, if the company is to grow and prosper, it's up to them.

Although risk agents serve as the core of the revolt, the agency includes others as well. Usually determined by the issue at the time, risk agents recruit others to join their movement. The recruitment of stable guard members provides tremendous power and protection for the agency. These are employees who have tenure (considered to be "lifers") and are seen by management as key to the stability of the org-

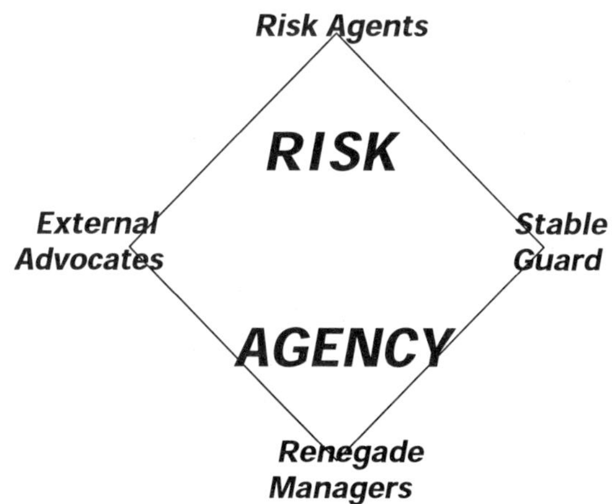

anization. They are extremely loyal to the company and their knowledge and experience of internal processes make them valuable to any successful challenge. The risk agency will also seek support from outside the organization. Influential players in the industry can often bring credibility and strength to the cause. Finally, the recruitment of some innovative and empowering renegade top managers (on a selective basis, usually revolving around a particular issue) can also bring strong allies to the risk agency. They bring the agency crucial information, knowledge, access to resources, and thus, power.

At the most basic level, the risk agency brings a new player to the table - a player with valuable chips which others around the table can not ignore. Although the size and strength of the risk agency will likely vary from time to time, it will serve as a permanent force in the organizational power arrangement.

Real Empowerment

If empowerment is to work, it is clearly up to the risk agent. As we have examined, top-down led empowerment has only been a fantasy. Few top managers have illustrated the confidence and the courage to "walk the talk." Therefore, if real empowerment is going to find a permanent footing in corporate America, the responsibility rests with risk agents and their agency. *Very simply, bottom-up empowerment is the only real option.*

Risk agents realize that traditional approaches to organizational problems and issues will not lead to real transformational change and improvement. Only a substantial adjustment in the power arrangement will allow for new and brave views toward organizational change. This new arrangement pits the risk agency against traditional management (or the so-called change agents). Our risk leadership model suggests that this unique bipolar struggle will eventually produce the positive change and growth desired for organizational success.

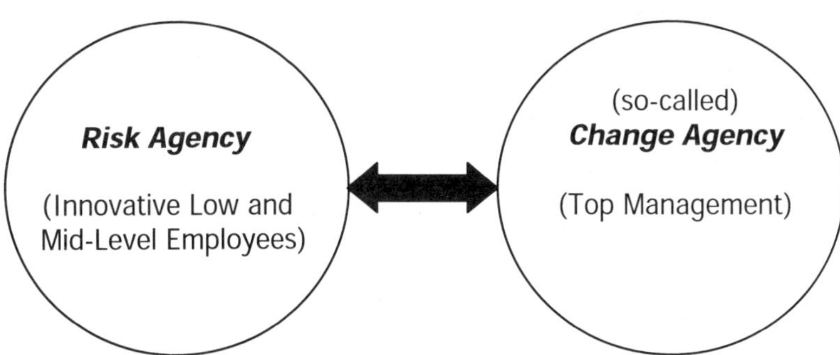

Risk leadership calls the risk agents to pressure the traditional change agency toward new and innovative solutions to organizational problems. Whether the revolt is motivated by a single issue, weakness of the leadership, or a transformational-driven challenge, the work of the risk agency follows three basic steps: *preparation, revolution, and resolution.*

First, risk agents must prepare adequately for the battle ahead. This includes assuming responsibility, assessing the organization, building a strong risk agency, and developing the alternative agenda. Next, risk agents must challenge, test, and to some degree, deny power to management. It must be recognized by all involved that there are limits to the power that leaders exercise. Risk agents do not follow them blindly; rather, they deny them unchecked power and the ability to ultimately make and implement decisions. Next, the risk agency confronts management. Here, risk agents simply say - NO! We have a better idea! Then risk agents, directly or indirectly, challenge authority. Whether behind closed doors or in open display, risk agents challenge the agenda (or the lack of) proposed by management. In turn, the risk agency recommends an alternative. The risk agency will work through the system, around the system, and even at times, subvert the system when necessary to carry positive change forward. Next, risk agents will often be required to activate conflict in order to have their vision and change plans adopted. Obviously, conflict (through non-violent acts) is neither easy nor comfortable. But without this uncomfortable strategy, management is not forced to recognize the new power arrangement, and thus, make serious changes. Finally, for the organization to avert

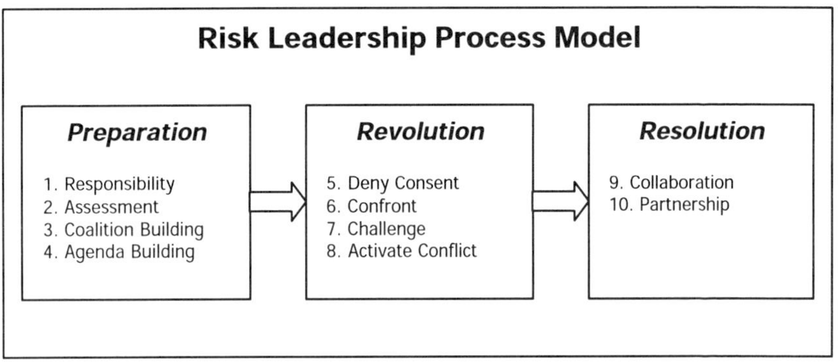

anarchy, both sides must compromise. It will become apparent to the risk agency and management that only by working together can real progress be made. Each is dependent on the other. Risk agents bring energy, innovation, and labor; while management brings the all-important resources to the table. This interdependence will demand collaboration.

A Risk Leadership Culture

The final phase of the process involves creating and institutionalizing the risk agency. There must be a major attempt to modify the traditional organizational culture into a culture that supports real empowerment, innovation, and change. Ultimately, risk agents must create an organizational culture that not only accepts confrontation and challenge, but expects it! Every effort must be made to create a permanent culture that recognizes internal revolt as a positive instrument of organizational progress.

The coalition of revolutionaries must find a way to make the process of confrontation and challenge an expectation. The ability to deny power, though seemingly simple, must be allowed and respected. The risk agency must work to institute processes, such as open forums or real TQM sessions, where confrontation can exist and be expected on a consistent basis. Successful revolutionaries must also be rewarded, and a way must be found to help the unsuccessful risk agents back to their feet after the TKO. Even when the risk agency fails, room must be made for their alternative views, otherwise factions and destructive cultures will prevail and take up where the risk agency left off.

Summary

Risk leadership proposes a dramatically new model for leadership, change, and organizational improvement. Built on a bottom-up confrontational approach, risk leadership encourages lower level employees to confront and challenge authority for the purpose of leading transformational change. Failures in the classical and progressive leadership approaches demand that we develop new power arrangements that will encourage organizational growth and success.

Risk agents will most likely be motivated to initiate and sustain internal dissent because of key organizational issues, the weakness of top management, or the failure of company transformation. Innovative risk agents then develop a "coalition of revolutionaries" who empower themselves and alter the power arrangement within the organizational structure. Through a series of revolutionary processes, the risk agency first challenges and then collaborates with management for the purpose of moving the organization forward. Finally, risk leadership calls upon all players to recognize the value of this unique approach and encourages the development of a permanent culture that allows for healthy confrontation.

MANDATE TO CONFRONT AND CHALLENGE

This section describes in detail the risk leadership model being proposed. Authors discuss the justification for the theory, who should participate, and what actions are needed to transform the organization.

Chapter 4

Justifying the Revolt: Motive to Confront and Challenge

Introduction

Every revolt has a catalyst that sets it into motion. Good or bad, every business revolt is based, to some extent, on the decisions of those in power. Motive, as it relates to shifting from classical and progressive leadership paradigms, is basic and crucial in building a case for risk leadership. As with any good prosecution in the courtroom, you too must have much more than a reasonable doubt to convict the criminal abuses of classical leadership and the negligent recklessness of progressive leadership.

Personal challenge, commitment, and change are all necessary elements to turn motive into action. These principles of personal motive are discussed given their strong relevance for initiating risk leadership. This section also focuses on the three main reasons why risk leadership occurs. Issue driven revolt is the first rationale discussed. Issue driven revolt comes from the risk agent's dissatisfaction with one particular policy or issue. Person driven revolt is further discussed as a possible motive. Person driven revolt occurs when the risk agency is concerned with a person rather than a particular issue or policy. Transformation driven revolt is elaborated and justified in light of the current failings of the classical and progressive models. Transformational change derives from the risk agency's overall lack of confidence in the status quo direction of organizational policies and management. Ultimately, something has to be done!

Every risk leadership confrontation is predicated on the ability of the risk agent to make sound and ethical decisions, and then influence others in the same manner. In this situation, the need for clear motive should not be underestimated. Motive drives the risk agent and those who join the risk agency. Without motive there is no common bond, and there is simply chaos against the establishment. Without clear motive, the risk agency puts its existence in grave jeopardy given the lack of underlying purpose. Any mobilizing event can spur conflict, but real change comes when the confrontation and challenge have been examined in light of conditions that have been well considered and cannot be denied.

Personal Motivation

Before beginning an issue, person, or transformation driven revolt, the risk agent must have personal desires and motivations which drive him or her to pursue the challenge. The process of defining and creating personal motive is relatively simple. Personal motive includes five connecting elements – realization, rationalization, refusal, reckoning, and reinforcement. One of the first elements of personal motivation involves a realization that a problem exists. This realization could also be a problem that may not be of crisis nature now, but may well be later. Furthermore, the risk agent may also realize that a situation could be improved without the recognition of a real "problem." Understanding the scope and nature of the problem is paramount to judging, acting, and finally influencing others to do the same. Often times the realization

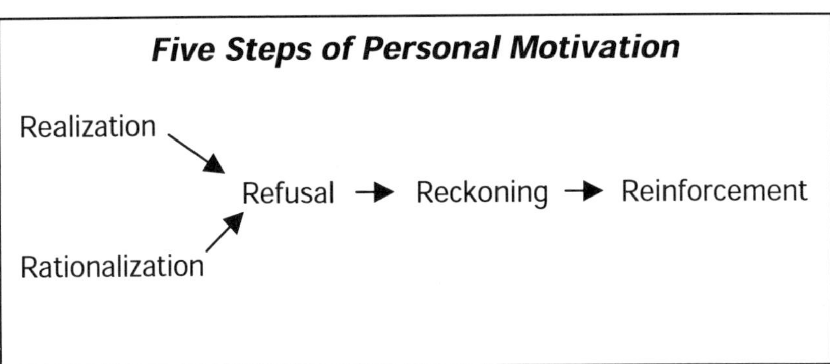

stage involves emotion and intuition more than actual thinking. There is much to be said about your own personal "gut feelings." Many times these impulses can spur us before the problem is of such magnitude that it is beyond our control.

For example, several risk agents in an east coast software company perceived that an organizational policy was inhibiting their growth rather than serving its original purpose. This company was creating Intranet applications for one particular healthcare organization. Three insightful people across several organizational levels realized that the product could be marketed to other healthcare organizations. This insightful realization translated into a major stop-gap funding source for the company while they were finishing a second release of the product for their primary client. This effort truly exemplified risk leadership because these individuals deviated from the executives' original "business plan," which meant steering the product just to the primary client. Foresight and market capitalization is, many times, hatched from the ideas and dreams of a few. Oaks grow out of acorns, so the adage goes.

Another primary aspect of initiating personal motive is the rationalization of the problem. Rationalization involves thinking about the causes, antecedents, effects, and manifestations of the problem. To rationalize does not mean that risk agents agree or approve, rather, that they understand the less than optimum conditions. During the rationalization stage, the risk leader seeks to understand more by talking to people. Realization may be done in relative isolation, but rationalization requires more than personal insights to be successful. The rationalization stage may be difficult for spontaneous risk takers. The last thing that some people want is details. But without thoughtful consideration, the risk agency will fail to accomplish the mission due to the lack of understanding critical details. Though not exclusive to small businesses by any means, this problem is evidenced by the plight of many small companies. Historically, approximately 50% of small businesses fail in their first year. One could easily speculate that the primary reason for their failure is the lack of research into market forces that were invisible to the entrepreneur at the time. Furthermore, it seems that no "business plan" in a large corporation is without serious setbacks. Without question, this happens due to a lack of research and rationalization of the forces that are influencing the problem. Better rationalization leads the risk agency out of the bunker and back onto the fairway.

Following the initial realization and rationalization, the risk agent engages in refusal - the right to stop the problem from existing any longer. At this stage the risk agent makes the assessment and determines that the problem is serious enough to warrant attention. This is a necessary and natural outcome of the realization and rationalization stages. Refusal should not be confused with strikes, job sit downs, or other similar workplace refusal behaviors. This stage is purely mental! It is at this stage that the risk agent "decides to decide" or makes the choice to build a strategy regarding the issue. Refusal is not to be confused with the actual decision or the behaviors that happen after the decision is made. Some may claim that this is a semantic and trivial difference, but the idea that people should decide to build strategy against the "enemy" is very reasonable and makes a great deal of sense if they are going to put their necks on the chopping block.

The next stage, the reckoning, is the actual decision making stage. Reckoning sounds formal and judgmental. It should be! When risk agents reconcile their attitudes about the problem, they are looking at the past, the present, and the possible futures to determine the best course of action. They may well consider the "perfect world" where no executives could shoot holes in their ideas due to management's short-sighted interests. In this strategy building session, risk agents should also consider those solutions that allow them to rally their forces. Risk agents want to see real solutions to real problems, not meager solutions and more business plans that skirt the real issues.

This stage is well displayed by a situation in a large insurance corporation. This firm had a difficult time implementing a software application developed in-house which was essential for Y2K compliance. As a result, a task force of key players from all parts of the organization was developed (from user, to developer, to project managers) and met to research possible problems and solutions. In the end, they reported strong and substantial findings which sent a shock wave throughout the company. They decided that ultimately they were at fault! As the stakeholders in the implementation process, they had not insured its success due to a lack of coordination and communication with all involved parties. While no one would loose their job over this announcement, it was a serious attempt at risk leadership given the multi-layered support, the frank honest truth, the desire to make right what was wrong, and the need to form a new agenda for the future. This agenda included detailed steps to overcome the weaknesses of organizational coordination. Following the task force report and ruffled feathers, the project went on to completion with a strong attempt from all parties to get past partisan infighting and reach a solution.

The final stage of the process of personal motive is the reinforcement stage. During reinforcement people actually talk themselves into the decision. True convictions result when people have decided and then go the extra step to commit to the decision. Reinforcement is the resolve that the risk agency exhibits. It is a "hardening of the attitudes" that makes others notice. Reinforcement is often the most visible part of the process because it is so public and so resolute. We can see examples of this in just about any workplace. People that act on their convictions have true motive and purpose. These people are often looked up to. If their cause is noble and serves the collective good, they become risk agents (and perhaps martyrs) for their cause.

Understanding the nature of personal challenge, commitment, and change is essential in order for understanding the motives of risk agents. Risk agents, as the basic unit of risk leadership, must go through the process personally before they can work through the process as part of the larger risk agency. The stages described are personal to the risk agent, whereas the stages of risk leadership represent the collective action of the entire agency. Without understanding the process that risk agents pursue to achieve personal commitment, there is little use talking about the reason why risk agents take on serious organizational problems.

The personal actions of risk agents are important because it is those very actions which drive the risk agent to revolt. This motive to revolt revolves around three primary reasons: issues, people, and organizational transformation. The next three sections isolate specific reasons why risk agents (and agencies) confront the status quo. Issue, person, and transformation driven revolts all begin with risk agents going through the processes of personal challenge, commitment, and change as described in personal motivation.

Issue Driven Revolt

Perhaps the most common reason that any change happens is that "it was a good idea at the time." Issue driven revolt centers around one or more business events that illuminate the building tension and frustration with the unworkable way of doing something. When tried and true business practices are worn out and antiquated, issue driven revolt becomes a option for some. Revolt based on an issue is usually a short-term commitment by the risk agency regarding one specific problem. If it extends beyond that issue to a broader indictment of the organization, then it should be considered transformational. It is very important to note that this type of revolt is a challenge of ideas, basic purposes, values, goals, objectives, and processes of a particular issue or policy. Issue driven revolt is not driven by division between people as much as it is driven by a division between ideas. That is not to say that issue driven revolt never takes on advocates for each side; in fact, it always does. The primary concern in this type of revolt is that the company could be better by improving a basic process, changing a policy, altering goals and objectives, or by looking at a fundamental assumption (idea) from a different direction. Thus, issue driven revolt comes from the perceived failure of a policy or process, rather than the failure of a person or the entire organization.

A good example for illustrating this type of revolt involves a small regional educational institution. There was widespread concern that one critical department was significantly low on resources. This concern was so troubling that a group of faculty members declared that they would forego pay increases that year in order to help the department if the administration would match those funds. There was clear reluctance on part of the administration to help the department in question. This issue was forced into an open forum where the faculty offer was publicly discussed. Ultimately, the administration buckled and gave the department more funding without taking pay increases from the faculty.

Person Driven Revolt

Person driven revolt happens when one person (or group of people, like executives or top management) force those without power to take notice. When classical leadership becomes so oppressive and when so much control exists at the top, differences become personal (not issue-based) and confrontation and challenge is imminent. Person driven revolt is divisive, separative, personal, and quite invasive. Person driven revolt is a real possibility when there is an extreme loss of faith in the leader or when the use of power is far beyond ethical. This type of revolt also happens when there is the belief that the leader is not competent enough to make the right decisions and choices.

Unfortunately, not all conflict is based on issues. There may be personal differences so great between workplace classes that revolt is the only way to control the controllers. Many personal differences exist between risk agents and top management. The sources are as varied as our personalities. Among the possible sources provoking challenge might include:

Sources of Difference for Person Driven Revolt

- Assumptions
- Attitudes
- Beliefs
- Behaviors
- Expectations
- Mission
- Policies
- Roles
- Values
- Vision

Person driven revolt can have dangerous effects on the organization. When a group of risk agents empower themselves to "bring down" a person at any cost, the results can be devastating. Before acting, the reasonable risk agent should seriously consider their motives and the possible effects on themselves, their agency, the company, and even the person in question. Of course, this is sometimes necessary when the leader's actions (or non-actions) threaten the success or even survival of the organization.

Recently, we had the opportunity to watch this very type of revolt happen in an organization with which we have been associated. A group of risk agents, fed up with the classical controlling leader in place, took steps to threaten the power base of that individual. Through formal and informal meetings, caucuses, hallway socializing, and arm-twisting, a consensus of several risk agents emerged that challenged and confronted the traditional methods of decision making used by the classical leader. When the classical leader took steps to delegitimize the risk agency, they struck back with legal and procedural actions that required outside institutional intervention. For many innocent bystanders these actions seemed to be based on issues, but for those parties involved it was personal. Hatred, anger, and extreme frustration are all hallmark of this type of struggle. The risk agency will only make inroads in this person driven revolt when their motives are driven by the collective concern of the organization. Rest assured, personal agendas will not die easily as long as the risk agency and the classic leader remain in their positions with different values and expectations.

Transformation Driven Revolt

The final type of risk agency revolution is transformative. One of the central goals of the progressive leadership movement has been to provide empowered people with the means to control and ultimately improve their workplace. In most cases this has not happened due to the methods of classical leaders. Classical and progressive leadership styles have not produced the successes that risk agencies demand. There is real reluctance to give up control of the key aspects of the business by classical and progressive leaders. Transformation driven revolt is seen as the way to eliminate the old culture of control and stability and rebuild a new environment based on the demands of the agency.

Transformational change happens when there is an unyielding frustration with the organizational values and culture. The attitude that "things should be better" grows, and there is a common feeling that real change must happen or the organization will collapse. Transformational change, if real and complete as referred to in Chapter 2, can have substantial impact on an organization. Transformational change is specifically used to make the organization better than before. It is our belief that the risk agency must take the power upon itself to make the changes necessary to insure organizational security and cultural improvement. There are several critical conditions (for classical, progressive, or risk leaders) that must be met in order for transformation to occur. Transformation driven revolt is not for the faint at heart, nor is it a process that will complete itself. Real transformational change is extremely difficult. This form of revolt is long-term and not just based on a limited intervention of one or two acts of the risk agency. Risk agents who have the ability to make transformational changes must be extremely dedicated and committed to their cause. Without that extreme level of determination, the process will be inadequate and the revolt may well fail.

Requirements for Transformational Change by Risk Agents

- Trust in the process and the people
- Genuine interest in a greater mission, purpose, and vision
- Eliminate fear and mistrust in all corners
- Fair, consistent, and constant assessment and evaluation of the process
- Commitment and follow through to the end
- Perseverance and determination
- Adaptable, responsive, and flexible
- No nonsense input and realistic assessment of the effects and results

One of the best examples of transformation driven revolt comes from the automobile industry. *General Motors, Ford,* and *Chrysler* had cornered the domestic automobile market for years. But domestic sales started slipping to less expensive and higher quality foreign cars. In the 1980s, *General Motors* took a bold step in trying to combat the tide of cars washing up on California beaches. *Saturn* became a product line that was not just innovative from an automobile standpoint, it also claimed to be a different way of doing business. The leadership of *General Motors* begrudgingly gave *Saturn* executives and line people power that they never had before to create a quality line of cars in which all parties had input into the process. Large corporations rarely make such bold and innovative moves without profit in mind, and *Saturn* has been just that for *GM* - profitable. While *Saturn* is probably more an example of successful progressive leadership, it took several risk agents much time and exhaustive effort to create such an endeavor. *Saturn* worked intimately with experts in Japanese management and Total Quality Management to create a domestic vehicle that competes with, and even beats, many foreign cars. Furthermore, the continued success of *Saturn* is built on the "power of one" to stop the assembly line and provide personal focus on quality. This type of company could not be built without risk agents forcing the issue and without continued confrontation and challenge when it comes to quality.

Summary

Most change occurs because someone is convinced that change needs to happen. Risk leadership is no different in this respect. However, risk leadership has specific processes and rationales motivating the change. Understanding the process of building a personal motive for change is important since the rationale for change is predicated on these actions. Likewise, personal motivation is rarely enough to make real change happen in an organization; therefore, other risk agents must be influenced. This process of personal motivation, and then influence, is often spurred by an important issue that cannot be pushed away any longer. In addition, there may be such impassioned disagreement disapproval over a leader's actions that a revolt based on personal characteristics is necessary. Furthermore, potential risk agents may be so frustrated over the whole system that transformation driven revolt becomes essential. Regardless of the driving force behind the risk agency, one must be constantly assured that there is thoughtful consideration of the facts, causes, and effects of the actions they undertake.

Chapter 5

A Coalition of Revolutionaries: The Risk Agency

Introduction

Risk agents are in a very unique position in the modern organization. Like Washington's troops crossing the Delaware for a surprise attack on the British, the risk agency quietly gathers its forces for swift and decisive action. Like the revolutionaries of that battle, the risk agency has everything to loose and just as much to gain. At stake, as in the battle over 200 years ago, is the organization in which they have invested their time, hard work, and emotion.

Risk agents are those who are simply frustrated with the performance and output of the organization. They are typically low and mid-level staffers who have a deep concern about the direction of their organization. Recognizing that they can not change and improve the organization on their own, they join others with shared concerns to develop a new power arrangement. This "coalition of revolutionaries," the risk agency, provide the risk agents with their best opportunity to impact future decision and implementation making.

While risk agents serve as the primary core of the revolt, the risk agency also recruits mercenaries from both inside and outside the organization. Some stable guard members, external advocates, and a few renegade top managers provide the risk agency with credibility and additional power. As an informal coalition, the risk agency seeks to achieve consensus among members, and thus, provides a united front as they challenge the status quo thinking of management. Whether mobilized by a single issue, the weakness of leaders, or the lack of transformational improvement, the coalition charges into battle with top management to produce organizational change.

In its most basic form, the creation and activities of the risk agency are overt processes to implement bottom-up empowerment. Knowing that classical and progressive leaders lack the will or interest to empower the troops, the risk agency must empower themselves. What separates risk agents from other internal dissention is their passion for the collective (organizational) good. What drives risk leaders is not self-interest or gain, but rather, overall organizational success.

Risk Agents: The Core of the Revolt

Risk agents, typically low or mid-level employees, are usually newer to the organization and are upwardly mobile. They are those in the organization that often find unofficial ways and processes to "get things done." Others describe them as people who think for themselves and "make things happen." Some would even argue that it is these unconventional thinkers who, when linked together across functional fields, are the producers for the company.

Most potential risk agent types share many common traits, skills, and attitudes about themselves and the organization. Risk agents are employees who are energetic, enthusiastic, and have a reputation for hard work and high performance. They are extremely capable, knowledgeable, and talented in their specialized field as well as having a good understanding of the organization as a whole. Co-workers see them as creative people who are always looking for new and better ways of doing things. They are innovative problem solvers who do not look for easy answers to complex organizational problems. They are also passionate about what they do and are persistent in pursuing what they believe to be right. Finally, risk agent types have strong collaborative and networking skills. They recognize that to be successful they must work closely with others in today's highly interdependent organizational structures. In many ways the successful risk agent is much like a special teams "go-to guy." They play the game well, have energy and enthusiasm for the club, and when it comes time to take charge, they do so without hesitation. Today's risk agent is ready to score points for the organization as their daily duty and stand ready to play the playoff game every time they step onto the organizational field.

Traits and Skills of Risk Agents

- Enthusiastic
- Energetic
- Hard Worker
- High Performer
- Knowledgeable
- Creative/Innovative
- Problem Solver
- Passionate
- Persistent
- Collaborator

While these traits and skills enable risk agents to confront and challenge authority, they are also the very qualities that give them organizational power and protection. Their reputation for high performance, for example, means they are seen as valuable to the organization. Ultimately the success of the organization rests with the input of these innovative and motivated employees.

In addition to these common traits and skills, many risk agents also share basic beliefs and attitudes which reflect their skepticism about the organization and its authority. Risk agents are frustrated with status quo thinking and behavior that is often widespread throughout the company. They are change and movement oriented and often resist the efforts that top management use to control them. In general, risk agents are critical of tradition and are less impressed and influenced by authority. They are seen by many as having that intangible, but undeniable, "can do" attitude. What separates risk agents from other high quality producers is their deep concern and interest for the collective good. They are truly driven by the need and desire to improve the organization as a whole.

Attitudes and Beliefs of Risk Agents

- Frustrated with status quo thinking and behavior
- Change and movement oriented
- Resist control efforts
- Critical of tradition
- Rarely influenced by authority
- Collective minded

The Risk Agency: Alliance and Coalition Building

To challenge authority and lead a successful transformation, a single risk agent cannot act alone. Even several risk agents operating on their own cannot survive against the weaponry of top management. What is needed is a "coalition of revolutionaries" who empower themselves to challenge and transform the organization as they battle their oppressors. Operating from the premise of "the power of many," the risk agency coalition creates a new competing power entity. The cross-functional risk agency provides its members with protection, as well as the means and power to change the organization. The coalition gives risk agents their best opportunity for success.

This informal cluster of risk agents is bonded together by three fundamental beliefs or assumptions. First, as a collective unit they believe that the organization should and could be better. They see that management, as well as their fellow workers, have simply accepted mediocrity. It seems everybody is just doing the minimum. Second, they have lost confidence in management's ability to successfully transform the organization. They believe that top executives lack the courage to make the difficult decisions needed to effectively lead the transformation. They believe it is time for managerial status quo thinking to go. Third, members of the risk agency believe they can and should take on the responsibility of directing and implementing organizational change. To them, if the organization is going to prosper, then they must get involved in the critical decisions and implementation processes.

Although a coalition can be difficult to create and maintain, it does offer a mechanism by which members can cooperate with each other as they pursue common objectives. Most successful risk agencies can be described as having highly committed members that are compatible with one other and are able to engage in free and open communication. Commitment includes not only acceptance of ideas, but also the willingness to act. Risk agents must be committed to their collective proposals as well as the overall purpose of the agency. Compatibility comes when agency members share basic assumptions about the organization and have a common interest in the goals of the coalition. Because agency members are often scattered throughout the organization (from the accounting department to sales to marketing), it is critically important that agency members communicate regularly. The most effective coalitions are described as having people who are able to routinely share ideas and coordinate activities. Finally, successful coalition efforts require credibility. Agency members must be able to trust one another as they collectively struggle against management.

In one example, a risk agency was allowed to develop and flourish within a service sector company. The organization was charged with the rapid development of a new and innovative service package for a government agency. Approximately 40 people worked on site, and another 10 worked off site as executives and marketers. It is our contention that this organization was able to successfully produce the needed product because of the risk leadership efforts of a small coalition. These people, though in different functional areas, kept in close contact, were highly committed to quality work, weren't afraid to speak their opinion and challenge management, and trusted the other members to do the same. As such, they created a unique and profitable service package that went beyond the organizational rules of the game. The final result was a product that defied the expectations and requests of management.

The strength and degree of cooperation among risk agents will also vary from time to time. Based on the issues and the need for coordination and resources, the risk agency may serve as a less formal network or alliance at one point and represent a more formal collaborative unit at another. At the less formal end of the continuum, risk agents operate in a looser or more flexible network environment where communication is less formal and the agency serves as a clearing-

Coalition Linkages

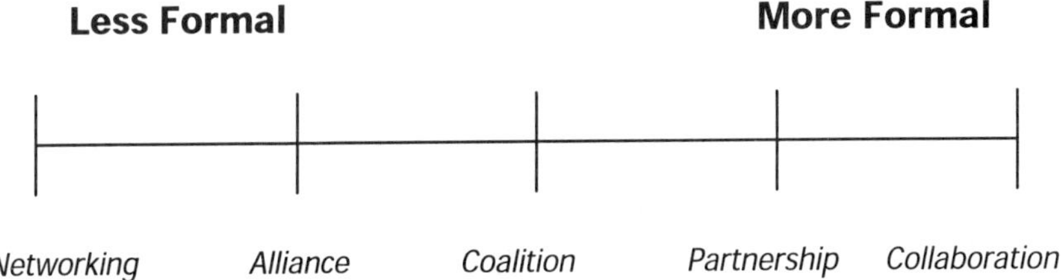

house for information and dialogue. Our example of the service sector company is an excellent case in point. This small informal coalition was able to succeed in the development and application of a service package by operating within a loose network. Most of their creations and solutions were acquired or obtained through late night brainstorming sessions. After everyone else had left the office, these risk agents stayed and shared ideas. By challenging bureaucratic policies and overcoming obstacles from management, they were able to produce a product that enhanced the collective good.

At the other end of the continuum, coalition members establish a much more formal structure. Here, consensus is used in decision making, communication links are highly developed, and individual roles are more formalized. For example, efforts to develop formal unions or collective bargaining units could be considered a higher-structured risk agency. What is important to remember is that there is no "correct" coalition arrangement. Organizational demands may require constant adaptation to the coalition structure. Thus, to be successful, risk leaders must alter the formality of the agency to fit the needs of each situation.

Revolutionaries: Risk Agents and Their Allies

The first step in developing a coalition is the recruitment of its membership. Eventually, the success of risk agency efforts will be measured to some degree by the size, cross-functional diversity, quality, and commitment of coalition members. At the core of the revolt is the risk agent. Risk leaders will need to seek out, identify, and recruit similar risk agent types throughout the organization. In most cases, they will provide the core resistance against management. They are the nucleus and leadership of the coalition. In many ways, the risk leader is like the rush party chair seeking to find the best match between external members (pledges) and a house.

In addition, the agency will also need to recruit others from both inside and outside the organization. First, the recruitment of some *stable guard* members will provide power and protection for the agency. These are long-term employees who are well established and are seen by management as providing stability for the corporation. They have favorable reputations and are loyal to the company. Stable guard members have knowledge and experience of internal processes, which makes them extremely valuable to any challenge effort. It is difficult to imagine an effective risk agency without the inclusion of a few stable guard members.

Next, risk leaders will need to seek support from *key players outside of the organization*. Influential consumers, suppliers, stock-holders, and community members, for example, can often bring tremendous strength to the cause. They add ideas, resources, new blood, and can be committed to the new results of the risk effort. Additionally, key professionals in the industry can add credibility to the risk agency. This alliance, more than any other, will make management take notice.

Third, the recruitment of some innovative and courageous top managers can also bring strong allies to the coalition. These *renegade lieutenants* may be tempted to join (or at least support) the risk agency on particular issues or agenda items. They bring the coalition crucial information, knowledge, resources, and therefore, additional power and strength. When they join the revolution, these brave officers carry legitimacy, authority, and privileged knowledge.

Traditionalists: Management and Their Allies

In the other corner are the traditionalists - top management (or as they call themselves, change agents). Without question, these executives feel directly threatened by risk agents and the risk agency. The generals will be surprised, confused, and even angered that these "lower-level" troops would and could challenge their authority. While some may respect their enthusiasm for the collective good, most will likely be offended by what they see as an overt challenge to their command and control structure. Some managers may seek to suppress the revolt, while others may simply seek to control it and re-direct its energy. Some see the renegade mercenaries as a direct threat to the operation and will find ways to honorably (or not so honorably) discharge them. The bottom line, however, is that top management will initially see risk leadership as a danger to the organization, and more importantly, their personal authority.

Management will not have to look hard to find allies. Although many company employees might be sympathetic to the revolutionaries and their cause, most will likely pursue safer roles and strategies. Because these employees seek stability and do not want to "rock the boat," they most often will support management's slower incremental processes.

In addition, every organization has what we call an "anti-change crowd." These are staffers across the organization who go to great lengths to fight any and all change efforts. At times they may see management as the enemy, but most often they will see risk agents and their change-dominated agenda as a threat to their comfortable day-to-day routines. The anti-changers can be easily mobilized by management to join the resistance against the risk agency.

Finally, while the risk agency may be able to recruit some stable guard members to selective issues or concerns, most will not want to risk their comfortable roles in the organization. Many have invested lifetime careers with the corporation and are not going to seriously damage their relationships with top executives. Therefore, top management will likely find quiet, behind the scenes, and experienced allies among the stable guard. When these important employees are linked with management, they can provide the so-called change agents with a lethal weapon.

Revolutionaries vs. Traditionalists

In their efforts to develop and maintain the coalition, risk agents will find themselves balancing the need for achieving internal consensus with their desire to initiate confrontation with outsiders. First, risk agents and their allies will need to reach a consensus on both their methods as well as the content of their proposed agenda. Providing a unified front will give the agency its best opportunity for success. In most cases, the structure of the risk agency will provide little formal decision making hierarchy. Risk agency members will have to continuously work together to achieve a consensus. Although disagreements are inevitable, finding common ground is more likely because agency members share many similar traits and attitudes about themselves and the larger organizational population.

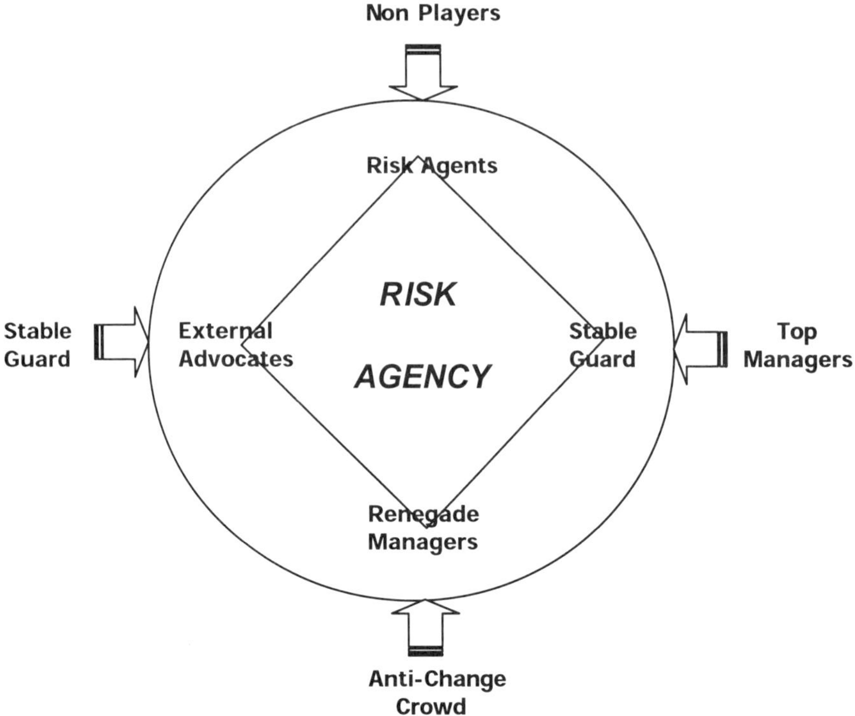

Next, the risk agency flexes its collective power. Once agency members agree on agenda items and strategies to win their acceptance, they challenge the organization's recognized establishment. This new power arrangement pits the revolutionaries against management and other traditionalists. The risk leadership model suggests that this unique bipolar struggle will eventually produce the positive changes needed for organizational growth.

Although this revolt is primarily directed toward top management, risk agency members will soon find several "confrontational points" around them. Battles will occur on several fronts over such things as loyalties, long-term and short-term agenda items, and revolt and implementation strategies. In addition to the confrontation with management, the risk agency will likely struggle day to day with non-players, stable guard members, and the anti-changers. Although these traditionalists will counter risk agents for reasons other than management, their resistance is just as frustrating for the coalition.

Each of these competing armies brings different forms of power to the conflict. Management utilizes their formal authority and their power over rewards, resources, and punishment to influence the outcome of the battle. This is not to say, however, that risk agents are limited in their ability to initiate and sustain bottom-up action. In fact, this new organizational arrangement calls for risk agents and the coalition to not only build, but also to exercise power as they confront management. Individual risk agents are likely to hold such personal power as strong track and performance reputations, knowledge and expertise, and control over vital information which allows them to influence others. More importantly, it is the development of the coalition that brings the heavy artillery to the battlefield. To some degree the risk agency can impact, or even control, the power of labor. More directly, subordinates can withhold, or even refuse, to implement management's agenda. Acknowledging that power is not equally distributed in modern organizations does not imply that privates and their sergeants do not have the power or the ability to influence the outcome.

Summary

In their efforts to implement bottom-up empowerment, risk agents develop a coalition of revolutionaries who together provide a unified front to challenge management. Risk agents are generally those employees who are not satisfied with the performance of the organization. They are energetic, innovative, hard working, and have deep interests and concern for the future of the organization.

By developing the risk agency, risk leaders and their allies build a new power entity, and therefore, alter the organization's decision making framework. Although the structure of the agency may vary in its formality, risk agents do share three fundamental beliefs: first, they believe that the organization could and should be better; second, they have lost faith in management's ability to lead the organization; and third, they believe that the risk agency can play an active role in promoting organizational improvement.

While risk agents serve as the core of the revolt, they enlist others in the agency who share common interests. This unique collective unit first seeks to find a consensus among members on important agenda items and then confronts and challenges the status quo arrangement. Risk leadership encourages the development of an uneasy confrontational relationship between revolutionaries and traditionalists for the purpose of discussing, debating and challenging ideas.

Often times, the risk agency views the organization as a prison. They believe the "establishment" within the prison is interested in one thing - command and control. But in most organizations, the risk agency realizes that they are not limited by the bars or by razor wire. We, as risk agents, have more power and freedom to create the product, service, and corporate culture that we would like. We are not goaded into behaving by cattle prods and bullwhips; rather, we have the control to make our risk agency the strongest force for advancement of the collective good.

Chapter 6

Shared Governance: Risking True Empowerment

Introduction

The concept of empowerment is not new to many organizational members, but its application is long overdue. In the modern organization, where empowerment is concerned, much ado has been made over nothing. Too often classical and progressive leaders have given inadequate efforts to empower their corps. Even when empowerment does occur, it is viewed as just another tactic or gimmick. True empowerment has been a mirage on the hot factory floor where the weary traveler becomes terminally frustrated with the journey.

Today's organizations face more critical problems than at any other time in history. Relations between management and line workers, while generally civilized, lack real substantive dialog. Historically, workers marched to save their rights; while today workers go to their cubicles and lick their wounds. Counter to the way that workers rose against *Carnegie, Rockefeller, DuPont,* and *Morgan* of the capitalist era, today's employees rarely demand to be empowered. Consider risk leadership as a call to arms, the rally cry, and the rebel yell for the unempowered to demand more from and for their organization. Today's complacent worker needs little more than the best interest of the larger organization and the will to achieve in order to become the fire that ignites the powder keg of risk leadership and bottom-up empowerment.

In attempting to move from the façade to real empowerment, we must critically examine the transition from past top-down attempts to our advocated bottom-up grassroots action. Furthermore, the process of working from the denial of power, to confrontation and challenge, to conflict and ultimately collaboration must be studied. Understanding the sometimes conflictive or congenial relationship between the risk agents and the change agents is also essential, just as is examining the evolution from conflict to collaboration. Finally, creation of the risk agency implies that a partnership of unparalleled mutual respect emerges over the long-term. This uncomfortable partnership is the ultimate expression of a perfect empowerment relationship in the risk organization.

Top-Down to Bottom-Up Empowerment: Walking the Talk

Saying "top-down empowerment" in most cases is like saying military intelligence or friendly fire. No matter how you say it, it just doesn't make sense. Top-down empowerment, as defined by many progressive leaders, is the ability of a leader to transfer power to the workers and to encourage widespread ownership of the process. Empowerment, even to the most liberal progressive leader, is still controlled by the top and done by those at the bottom. To think that top management would willingly give power to those who could use it for their own will (even if it is the same as the organizational will) is to be naive at best, or delusional at worst.

Progressive leadership viewed empowerment as an attractive alternative to the delegation tactics of classical leaders. The ability to empower is not derived from the same power base which delegation comes from, but in many cases the motive and the results are similar. Progressive leaders used more referential power (the power embodied in positive relationships with the corps), while classical leaders used more rudimentary forms of power like reward, punishment and legitimacy (formal power based on the authority of the leader's title/position). For classical leaders the motive is to increase efficient production, for the progressive leader it is to leverage the fullest motivation from the employee. Under the progressive style, empowerment gains have been short-term at best, and have been achieved at the expense of respect and trust.

The failure of prior forms of empowerment can be traced to one primary root source - upper management's control of the empowerment process. Empowerment, as defined under the risk leadership model, does not have power and control as the one unifying tie that binds the desires of top management with the hard work of employees. Power and control, central to the processes of the classical and progressive leaders, are antique and inappropriate for long-term growth of an organization. Like risk agents, top management too must understand that power and control is "business as usual," while empowerment approaches should be anything but that. Giving up power for many classical and progressive leaders is not easy. Giving the "keys to the company" to those who have the least invested was thought to be heretic and suicidal. Today, however, many would argue that denying important decision making power to lower employees would be just as suicidal. All members of the organization have a role to play. To empower is simply unlocking the chains that have bound the workers to their cubicle and management to their boardrooms. Both parties are finally liberated to do the real business at hand.

So what is bottom-up empowerment? *As risk agents know, true empowerment comes when power, control, and authority is wrestled away from top management and distributed to those who can use it to make real improvements.* Top management simply does not give away their power; true empowerment demands bottom-up action. Nor can you walk into the boardrooms across America (and beyond) and say, "please may we have some, sir." Quite the contrary, bottom-up empowerment comes when we deny power to those who wield it. In his book titled *Leadership*, James MacGregor Burns suggests that the wielders of power lack the ability or real interest to transform their organizations. Once power is denied, those who really want empowerment confront the status quo and say, "enough is enough." A rally cry that rang round the country during the 1992 presidential election was "it's time for them to go." No more business as usual. Confrontation is based on the challenge of ideas; it is issue driven, based on ineffective personal attributes, or even more important, driven by a strong desire to make a lasting change in the way the organization operates. Empowerment emerges from this conflicting arrangement. Challenge may often cause open and active conflict over the way things need to get done. Finally, from this dialectic tension comes a truce between warriors. Collaboration brings the empowerment process full circle. This new culture places all organizational parties on a more equal playing field. Therefore, bottom-up empowerment provides the model that truly unlocks the potential of all employees.

Preparation: The Keys to an Effective Revolution

Preparing for revolution is no easy task. Preparation is marked by a necessity for the risk agent to *assume responsibility.* As risk agents assume responsibility they imply that the organization is generally failing. This may involve some issue that is so troublesome that it cannot go unresolved or the fact that some person is hurting the organization too much to continue unchecked. Assuming responsibility takes place at two levels. First, risk agents take on a personal responsibility for themselves. Personal responsibility is much like any other internal standard or expectation that we might place on ourselves. When we assume personal responsibility, we are really proclaiming that we can no longer accept things the way they are for our own peace of mind. Personal responsibility, like a conscience, is a serious driving force for risk agents.

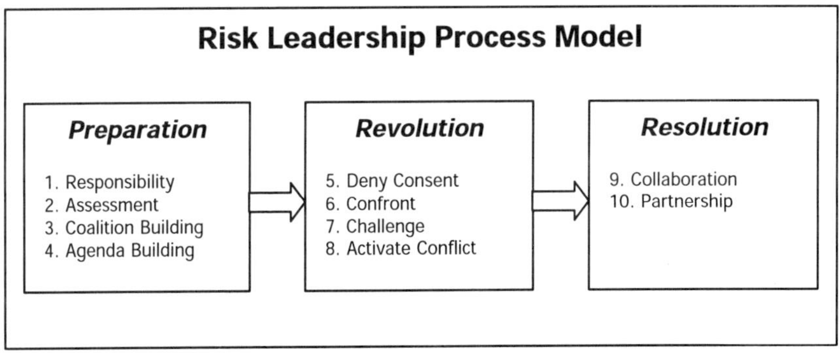

Without some level of personal responsibility and motivation, real change will not happen. Personal responsibility and motivation is the first thing that differentiates risk agents from other organizational members. The realization that something must change is one of the most important precursors to effective risk leadership and real bottom-up change. Assuming personal responsibility involves investing time, effort, and credibility.

> ***Strategy 1: Assuming Responsibility***
>
> When risk agents personally assume responsibility, they first recognize that all is not well, and second, that it is personally up to them do something about it. When assuming organizational responsibility, risk agents are motivated by their drive to serve other organizational players as well.

The second type of responsibility centers more at the organizational level. When assuming personal responsibility, it is more about the individual connection with the organization. When assuming organizational responsibility, risk agents show interest and concern for their coworkers. Organizational responsibility ultimately states that risk agents must improve the organization, not only for themselves, but also for those around them as well. Risk agents realize that the organization is not self-repairing and that issues, key personnel, and general organizational failure may hinder the organization from reaching its fullest potential. They believe that they can and should make a difference to benefit all parties. Therefore, risk agents assert themselves and take ownership in the organization. While the assumption of personal responsibility is likely to be more private, assuming organizational responsibility will likely be public. Once risk agents take this overt step forward, others will take notice.

Organizational assessment, as the second part of preparing for risk leadership, is important for the long-term success of both the risk agency and the organization. When assessing the organization, they are really trying to understand more about the issues and problem areas of concern. There are a variety of ways to assess an organization. One of the most common is to learn more about the views of other organizational members. This includes non-threatening conversations, in-depth interviews, and the formation of focus groups. These are just a few examples of where and when risk agents can assess the opinions of others and gather information and perspectives about the issues, people, and general organizational condition. Other methods not to be overlooked include hard statistical data on the organization's market share, productivity levels, and profit margins, for example. When assessing the organization, one must focus on the strengths, weakness, threats, and opportunities that the organization currently and will likely face in the future. Any successful assessment must examine the positive as well as the negative aspects of the organization.

One of the most important considerations in the assessment process is the ability of the researcher to remain objective. Objectivity is critical for the success of the risk leadership effort. Too often, we assess others just to hear what we want to hear. This is not acceptable! Without objectivity, risk agents loose the true perspective in favor of their own untested and unconfirmed views. Loosing objectivity can easily be fixed by stepping back and listening to what the informant has to say. Objectivity is perhaps one of the key obstacles to overcome for an effective assessment process. Utilizing multiple assessment methods will provide risk agents with the most realistic and accurate conclusions.

Strategy 2: Organizational Assessment

Assessing both the strengths and weaknesses serve as the foundation for any transformational change. When risk agents assess their organization, they methodically and objectively gather information about the issues and problems that are currently faced by the organization.

The third part of preparing for risk leadership involves *building coalitions* among people who share the same opinion regarding the issues, people, and organizational problems of concern. Coalition members share many of the same attitudes and beliefs about the organization and its need for transformational change. Without a coalition, risk agents have little power to enforce their collective will on the organization. As in many other situations, there is strength in numbers. As discussed in Chapter 5, building a coalition is based on the beliefs that the organization can and should be better, that management has failed, and that they should take the responsibility for directing and implementing organizational change. A coalition is committed to working toward their common objective through commitment and collaboration.

At this stage of the process they may lack a developed consciousness about their true direction, but that will come soon.

One of the defining characteristics of a coalition is its ability to be linked together by a common concern for the collective good of the organization. The act of linking comes in many different forms, but risk agencies generally progress from a less formal linkage to a more formal structure. Early on risk agencies can be described as having less formal linkages which involve mainly networking and alliance behaviors. As the risk agency matures around a common goal, they will likely develop a more formal coalition structure. As they reach this final stage of maturity, risk agents become partners and collaborators.

Strategy 3: Building a Coalition

When risk agents build a coalition, they are joining forces with others who hold similar beliefs. As the coalition develops, risk agents begin to collaborate to achieve their goal.

The final part of the preparation stage occurs when the coalition of risk agents finds a common direction and purpose. *Forming an agenda* is a central component for advancing to the real work of the risk agency - the revolution. The risk agency must fully understand the issue, person, or need for transformation in order to create a vision for a successful risk leadership effort. The risk agents must achieve consensus on this directive agenda prior to actually engaging in the revolution. Failing to gain a consensus at this stage would put the revolt in peril, and the risk agency would soon fall apart once denial of power and confrontation occurred.

It would not be uncommon for the risk agents to come out publicly at this stage almost as a pseudo-warning for management. Once their position is set and committed to, public acknowledgement is a small step in the process of starting the revolution. It is important that risk agents have a strong personal commitment to the mission and vision before making a public statement of their beliefs.

A final consideration at this stage relates to the leadership process within the risk agency. Productive risk agents cannot be led the same way as top management has attempted to lead them. When building the risk leadership coalition, it is important that risk agents allow shared leadership among all competent parties involved. As they strive to achieve consensus on the issue, person, or organizational malaise, risk agents must strive to keep all members of the coalition involved in the process. Risk leaders must learn from the mistakes of top management and lead others in a manner that considers the individual and the organization, not just the bottom line.

Strategy 4: Forming an Alternative Agenda

Risk agents build a coalition around a mission and vision. Building consensus on the issue, person, or organizational problem is essential to forming an alternative agenda.

Revolution: Denying Power and Confrontation

Recognizing the unique power that the risk agency and risk agents possess is only part of the process. True risk occurs when the revolutionaries decide to exercise that power by influencing and persuading their colleagues. The first part of the corporate revolutionary process involves a radical departure from the way that people have traditionally responded to top management.

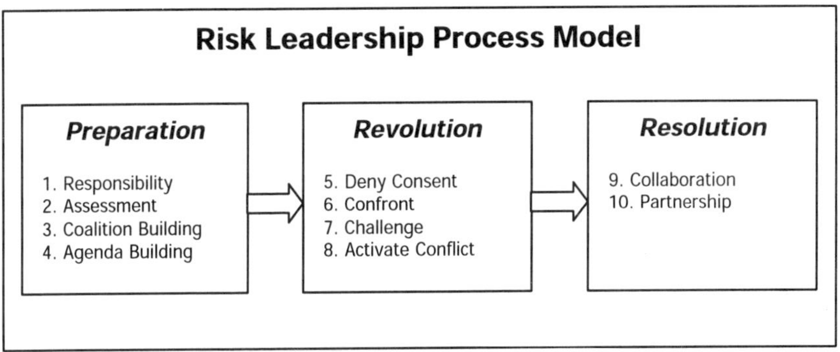

The first step in the revolutionary process is the *denial of power*. This process starts when a risk agency takes the ultimate stand by stating, "this can be no more!" The so-called change agents are naturally surprised by this stance, but realistically it should be no surprise. Denial of power is forcing the same power back on those who attempt to use it. The risk agency, with all their strength, is willing to take the stand on the one important issue, person, or systemic change that matters. Their position is so resolute and steadfast that denial is the obvious step in the process. When they exercise the denial of power, the risk agency is taking the first, and perhaps the largest, risk that their coalition may face. The denial of power represents the proverbial line in the sand that informs top management of the limits of their abuses. Denial of power is the break in tradition that takes the risk agency beyond the point of no return.

Strategy 5: Denying Power

When risk agents deny power, they stop the cycle of abuse by refusing to be a part of the problem any longer. The risk agency says "no more" and acts according to their mission rather than the directives of top management.

In one case we observed, denial of power was the central feature the risk agency used to gain legitimacy. Initially, risk agents were not able to build the coalition needed to deny the power of the chief executive. As a result, the risk agents were simply whisked out the door and little happened. As the coalition built strength, risk agents began to flex their muscle. In following instances in which the CEO was denied consent to govern the empowered risk agency, the results proved to be more impressive. Finally, on one particular occasion the CEO was denied power over salaries of the professional employees. The professionals invoked collective bargaining, thus curtailing the control that the CEO had over the issue. The CEO, a typical classicist, responded in defiance of the risk agency and their call for collective bargaining by citing loopholes. However, the CEO was finally forced to recognize and acknowledge the new organizational power arrangement. Ultimately, the risk agency gained additional advocates and strength due to the denial of the power of the CEO and the resulting actions.

Confrontation is a natural extension of the denial of power process. Confrontation occurs when top management tests the line; they attempt to escalate their response in an effort to match the denial of power of the risk agency. Often top management is surprised, even though they shouldn't be, by the defiance of company policy, personnel, or the organizational culture. The risk agency is simply saying "enough is enough" and denying the top management the ability to use power to force a result. It is at this point in the process that management understands that the risk agency is real and not going away without considerable attention. Both the risk agency and top management want to show the other "who the boss is". Denial of power is a great step, but if management tests that resolve and the risk agency caves in, then top management is back to the same stature, or better, than before the denial. When the revolt enters the confrontation phase, top management knows that the denial is real and that the risk agency has every intention of fulfilling its mission of resolving an issue, addressing a personality problem, or reforming the organization. The confrontational risk agency, when pushed, does not back away from the fight. Rather, they consider the issue involved and create a rational challenge to the provoked response of top management.

As mentioned earlier with our example in Strategy 5, the denial of power by the risk agency led to the next revolutionary process - confrontation. It was at this stage where the CEO began to take the risk agency seriously and resolved to fight them. During the confrontation stage, the CEO became even more hostile than earlier in the process. This seems normal since the CEO believed that the risk agents had less power, while at the same time were not willing to back down. It was at this point, under fierce pressure from top management, that the risk agency did not yield. The CEO found a steadfast, resolute, unyielding risk agency. Emotions flared and decision making suffered, but the risk agency was able to maintain composure and avoid loosing resolve in the first real threat to their revolt.

Strategy 6: Confrontation

Confrontation occurs when top management demands a return to status quo, and the risk agency responds with their steadfast denial of power. Confrontation escalates the denial to make the risk agency stance real to top management.

Of central importance to the successful risk agency is the ability to *challenge* the issue, the people, and even the organization. As argued earlier, this challenge may be open or covert, it may be direct or subtle, or may even be friendly or hostile. Regardless of the angle taken, the challenge is a very important part of the process, given the lack of rational exchange of ideas up to this stage. The challenge stage is where the risk agency uses a rational argument (with supporting data) to officially propose their alternative agenda.

A challenge of issues is not that substantially different from a challenge of the person or the corporate transformation. When the risk agency challenges the issues put forth by top management, they are in fact challenging the ideas which those issues promote. In order to really understand the issue, the risk agency must critically examine the history, causes, and effects of the issue. Furthermore, when the risk agency challenges an issue or policy, it is prudent to look at all of the implications surrounding that particular subject. It is also important to recognize all of the players involved in the challenge. Each of us has friends and foes, and sometimes challenging an issue makes for strange bedfellows in the end.

Issue driven challenge must focus on a particular policy, directive, decision, or rule that gets in the way of the organization becoming more than it is. This type of challenge is generally so centered on one policy that the risk agency lives and dies as the issue waxes and wanes. It is important to note that the risk agency can (and probably does) take on other issues, but there are "one hit wonders" that have one salient issue. When a risk agency takes on issue after issue, one might correctly wonder if they are more involved in a transformational challenge rather than an issue driven challenge. This may well happen, but there are different dynamics that drive both. The final element of the issue driven challenge is the severity of the issue. For a risk agency to be successful, the issue should be one of real importance to the organization. Picking the right battles to win is very critical to the overall success of the risk agency. Taking on top management on issues that are unimportant trivializes the process of risk leadership and lessens the chance for future success for the risk agency. One might easily advise the risk agency to "pick the battles small enough to win or big enough to matter."

Challenging people without challenging the person is even more difficult, but nonetheless important in many cases. In every organization there are people that detract the organization from its mission. There are times that certain top managers simply do not match their organizations. Whatever the case, challenging the people involved is tricky and too personal for many risk agents. When a risk agency challenges a person they are essentially saying that there is "no confidence" in the leadership abilities of the person in question. This challenge should remain focused on the issues and the behaviors, not the feelings and emotions of the person being challenged. Person driven challenge is not a witchhunt of an unpopular leader. Rather, the person driven challenge should seek genuine change primarily of the leader, with restructuring or removal as a secondary solution. To keep the challenge out of the realm of personal attack, the risk agent must be constantly reminded that, like themselves, everybody plays a role in the grander organizational scheme. Stalinist purges do organizations no good, and people centered challenge is useful if the behavior of the person is changed, not necessarily if the person is just removed.

The final type of challenge evolves when risk agents find the situation so dismal that drastic change is seen as the only alternative to save the organization. As previously noted, transformation driven change occurs when the conditions are so pathetic that systemic change is necessary. Transformational change is contrasting to issue driven revolt where just one particular policy or issue is in need of change. Total systemic change, rather than incremental change, is essential to the life of the company in many cases. In these not so rare situations, the risk agency must undertake perhaps the most difficult form of challenge - challenge of the entire system. Due to its complexity, transformation driven challenge must be developed with a clear purpose and vision in mind when the risk agency begins its process. To think that transformation is something less than a massive effort in an organization is delusion. Believing that transformational challenge involves a small change here and a tinker there truly understates the real mission of the risk agency. Furthermore, to think that changing the role of one person is true transformation is equally naive. Challenge based on the system comes only from exhaustive and competent reflection on the totality of the issues and problems surrounding the organizational environment. Understanding each partisan is important; although, transformation driven challenge calls for a unified change of all partisans, rather than a challenge to small issues within each specialty.

Strategy 7: Challenge

In the challenge stage the risk agency takes a stand against the issue, person, or larger organizational problems by advancing to rational argumentation. The challenge stage is more objective than the other stages, given its insistence on ideas rather than on pure emotion as in the previous stages.

Risk agents and the so-called change agents differ in several basic ways. Like oil and water, they do not mix. Risk agents are interested in immediate change in the circumstance that precipitates their emergence. These so-called change agents are more interested in slow controlled change that is planned and monitored for progress. Their motives may be the same to some limited extent - a better organization - but their route to that goal is quite different. Most top managers are interested in consolidating their own power base and controlling those around them. Given the differences it should be expected that some level of conflict is not only possible, but inevitable. The two organizational parties are now introducing competing and diverse agendas. The challenge stage places the risk agency in a direct collision path with a current policy, person, or system. Resultingly, conflict naturally emerges from this challenge. *Conflict is the protracted discussion over the merits of the issue or issues of concern.* It is not only common to have disagreements over the basic assumptions behind the two competing agendas, but it should be expected. This conflict frames the central issues for the organization and provides the foundation for true organizational change. Risk agents should not fear conflict; rather, they should embrace and encourage disputes over the real substance of the risk agency mission. Conflict builds from four basic sources: emotion, ideas, inequality of resources, and procedure.

Conflict emerging from emotion is notably present when risk agents feel bitter, angry, or fearful about the lack of change. Obviously, these feelings are manifested in the denial of power, challenge, and confrontation. In turn, it is equally probable that those who hold the power feel so impassioned about the challenge to their authority that they react to the opposition. This may lead both parties away from the real issues and into the realm of "negative fantasy" where they imagine and plan for the worst, rather than focusing on the reality of the situation. Risk agents should be cautious of basing their challenge on the emotional response to the policy rather than their ultimate objective. The challenge and conflict stages must be based on the real issues and policies of the opposing agendas. One cannot expect top management to back out of a policy change due to rising emotion, but one could expect a better response if reasonable discussion occurs after the denial of power. It is important to note that the best risk leaders are those who can control their emotions. When risk agents base their argument solely on emotional appeals, they may often inflame the situation beyond repair.

The second and most productive source of conflict is one based on ideas or positions. Risk agencies that focus on ideas, issues, policies, and similar elements of the corporate landscape are likely to be more successful given their ability to focus on tangible outcomes, rather than the emotional status of the risk challenge. Conflict based on issues is relatively sterile in comparison to affective conflict. For organizational success, both parties must be able to set aside their personal emotions from the conflict and focus on the real issues. Rest assured that this sterile situation will still have enough emotion to enable risk agents to sustain the challenge. An example of this type of conflict could be seen when management and employees disagree about the best way to make the company more responsive to a changing environment. Top management may feel that cutting the "tenured" employees is the best way to make the company more responsive. While employees may feel that through normal attrition the same objective can be met. There is a basic difference in opinion on this issue, and obviously there is more than enough passion to keep this important issue on the front agenda. Ultimately, idea dominated conflict provides the risk agency with its best opportunity to be recognized and taken seriously by the so-called change agents.

Conflict over unequal resources is very troubling to many risk agents for obvious reasons. When one department is singled out as the favored and other departments bear the costs associated with that favoritism, it is easy to understand why risk agents mobilize. Often resources are a major point of contention in times of feast or famine. Many employees are very interested in why others may receive more resources at their expense, while wealthier departments are interested in maintaining their stature. Conflict based on unequal resources, like conflicting ideas, is best if it remains on the course of the factual rather than the emotional. Just as is the case with conflict based on ideas and issues, there are likely to be more than enough polarized emotions to sustain the risk agency.

The classic example of this type of conflict happens when a sales department is allocated more resources simply because "they produce." When purchasing, distribution, accounting, and customer service see that one department is favored, there will be rumbling. When a coalition of dedicated employees challenges top management and the sales department, then risk leadership is afoot. The alternative agenda is simple: pay all people for the value they add to the production cycle. Conflict is destined to occur, since people want to keep their perceived portion of the pie. A note of caution: risk agents must be very careful when they mobilize over money. If there is inequity of resources, it is important to keep the collective good as the focus rather than what is good (or bad) for one partisan or another. Without focusing on the collective or common good, it is impossible to achieve any sustained consensus.

The final type of conflict emerges over procedure. In many ways this type of conflict may be the underlying reason behind most risk agencies. When management makes decisions in autocratic ways, as commonly happens, this non-participation drives the risk agency to seek power. If top management makes authoritarian demands on employees, then employees can in turn legitimately make the decision to deny them power and engage in the risk process. Conflict over procedure is generally not the only reason to mobilize a risk agency. Often times, there are issues that add fuel to the fire. The manner in which decisions are made is just as important as what is decided.

Strategy 8: Activating Conflict

Conflict is the protracted discussion over the conflicting agendas being proposed by the risk agency and top management. This conflict may build from four basic sources: emotion, ideas, inequality of resources, and procedure.

What we espouse may be motivated more by procedure, given the silent and often hidden oppressive nature of the lack of participative decision making. The risk agency is fighting for their *input* regarding the important issue, not just the issue itself. What is at stake in this form of conflict is the ability of the risk agency to say "the next time you try to make an autocratic decision for us, you'd be best served by asking for our input." Furthermore, the risk agency will most often take issue with decisions that were made without their input. Even if the decision is something with which they might have agreed, the risk agency views the decision as suspect. A good example of this sort of conflict is seen any time that top management makes policy decisions that affect the employees without their input or consideration. Conflict over procedure can also happen if top management looks to just a few unrepresentative employees to support their position.

Resolution: Collaboration and Partnership

To move the risk agency and top management beyond confrontation, challenge, and conflict may seem to be a miracle in itself. However, this final transition is critically important to the long-term

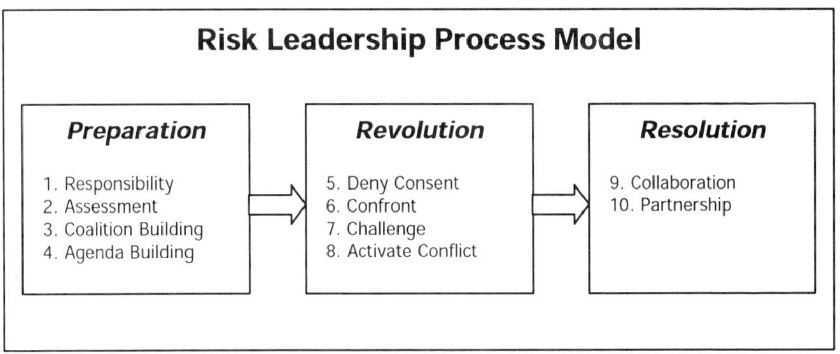

success of both the risk agency and the organization. No organization can stay in the conflict stage forever. Risk agents and top managers must find a common ground in order to avoid continuous discord. They need to recognize that collaboration requires a substantial commitment from both parties. The risk agency and top management must buy into a joint outcome and be committed to the long-term success of the company in order to have a chance at real change. Believing in the process and the content of the decision is essential in order for *collaboration* to occur. One should also be reminded that the easiest path to success is not always the best.

There are two basic ways that organizations resolve the dispute. One road is through compromise and the other is collaboration. The first way occurs when both parties simply get so tired of the confrontation, challenge, and conflict that one gives in to the other. This, as implied above, is compromise. Compromise in many situations is a positive thing. For example, compromise is the driving force behind our capitalist economy - "driving a hard bargain." However, compromising in a situation where you stand to loose respect, dignity and all the hard work you put into denying power, confronting authority, challenging issues, and engaging in conflict is indefensible. It could be argued that compromise, in this context, results in loosing more than the actual effort it took to engage in the process. Under these circumstances, the next risk leadership attempt would likely be met with moans and groans of "nothing happened last time, why should we do anything this time." We can even argue that a weakened risk agency that compromises their basic mission could over the long run self-destruct. Compromise happens when the fight overpowers the risk agency's will to continue. Exhaustion sets in and we loose steam. Eventually, the agency withers before the final hurrah.

The second type of resolution is that of collaboration. Collaboration seeks an outcome that is win-win for both parties. Collaboration is dependent on the ability of the risk agency and top management to set their differences aside for the sake of the organization. Thus, collaboration is for the collective good of all. In many ways it goes beyond the priorities of each party to outcomes larger than were possible when the risk agency originated. Collaboration requires both players to be active participants in the decision making process. In order for collaboration to occur, risk agents and top managers must have a mutual recognition of their opponents' value to the organization. Top management must accept the role of the risk agency as the arbiter of reality, and the risk agency must accept top management's formal role in the organization.

Strategy 9: Collaboration

Collaboration is dependent on the ability of the risk agency and top management to set their differences aside for the sake of the organization. Collaboration occurs when both parties concede mutual viability and activate change for the collective good.

Collaboration, like challenge and conflict, poses its own risks for both sides. The risk agency must invest their sum worth to create a solution that addresses the issue, the person, or comprehensive change of the organization. They risk their legitimacy, respect, and the informal power relationships they have worked so hard to foster. Top management, on the other hand, risks resources, legitimacy, authority, and their ability to stop the process (stability). Top management has the most resources to offer and the most stability to loose, but the risk agency also has many intangibles they stand to forfeit. Therefore, both parties must actively seek an outcome that is mutually agreeable.

Finally, to ensure future growth and success of the organization, both the risk agency and top management will need to develop a *long-term partnership*. The risk leadership arrangement requires that these two opposing power entities form an "uncomfortable" partnership that is based on confrontation. Positive change occurs when competing views are debated and discussed, and ultimately a collaborative outcome is reached.

The most important element in this partnership is the dialectical tension between the risk agency and top management. Without this tension, both parties will declare victory and rest on their accomplishments. If left alone, top management will revert to control, stability, bureaucracy, and efficiency. Likewise, without a controversial issue, the risk agency becomes hollow and pointless, drifting with no purpose. Together, the risk agency and top management create a relationship where both parties challenge and confront the other with the expressed purpose of creating positive change for the long-term. Dialectic is best achieved when opposites collide and show stark contrast between each other. Differences of opinion about issues, people, and the overall direction of the organization create a divide so great that only real consensual agreement can possibly bridge the gap.

Top management is focused on keeping change to a minimum, maximizing profits, and in most cases, squashing the risk agency. Their version of the collective good is "what's good for management is good for the company." On the other hand, the risk agency is out to make a name for themselves. Their main focus is to become the thorn in the side of management and to fight any roadblock that stands in the way of positive change. Their role is one of adversary of both the process and the greater issues involved. The risk agency's version of the collective good is quite common and focused on the larger constituency. As a partner in the process, their role is to be an advocate for change which benefits collective good. They serve as the voice of reason to the steadfast controls of top management.

Strategy 10 - Creating an Uncomfortable Partnership

The risk leadership arrangement requires that risk agents and top managers form an uncomfortable partnership that is based on confrontation. Positive change occurs when their alternative agendas are debated and discussed, producing an outcome which benefits the collective good.

This partnership is one of discomfort; however, the benefits to the organization are so great that both parties would feel justified in their positions. When one side flexes its muscle, the other side flexes back. When one side is offended, the other side claims victory. In this uncomfortable partnership, both parties are stakeholders in the outcome of the greater organizational success. These organizational governors -

the self-proclaimed and the bureaucrats - serve at the will of the organizational good.

Summary

Risk agents have a daunting task. Their job is to guard the organizational integrity without the firepower to do it well. At stake is their ability to be a force for the collective good and to fight against the withering decay of status quo thinking and stop-gap incremental change. In their quest to become key players on the organizational playing field, they must empower themselves, stand up to the establishment, confront and challenge ideas, take sides against a worthy enemy, and finally, find a way to put aside differences to further the collective good.

The process of bottom-up empowerment, from its confrontational start to the collaborative ending, is tiring, troubling, and fraught with disaster at every turn. However, if empowerment is to be, then there is no alternative to this proposed bottom-up revolutionary action. Initially, risk agents must prepare for the good fight. They need to assume responsibility, assess the organization, build a supporting coalition, and create an alternative agenda. Next, the agency must engage in the revolutionary processes of denying consent, confronting authority, challenging ideas, and then activating conflict with top management. Finally, risk agents and their supervisors must seek a collaborative outcome which benefits all organizational parties. This includes the development of a long-term partnership between competing forces.

The risk leadership model provides not only the framework for true bottom-up empowerment, but also the justification for doing so. The old ways of managing are over. Stability and control are no longer acceptable in today's modern organization. At stake is shared leadership, real transformational change, and outcomes that truly benefit the collective good.

EMPLOYING THE REVOLUTIONARY MANDATE

This section describes the strategies required for you to implement the risk leadership model. The authors provide the practical "how to" processes of preparation, revolution, and resolution.

Chapter 7

Preparation: The Gathering Clouds

Introduction

Talking about risk leadership is one thing, but doing it is quite another. Risk leadership is challenging and complex. Engaging in risk leadership will be the most difficult part of your job. The difficulty comes from the fact that you will be called upon to do a job that you have never done before. You will required to initiate the uncomfortable process of confrontation. Walking into risk leadership is like walking on hot coals to display your faith...you have seen others do it and succeed (fail too), but you are not sure if you have the right stuff to get the job done. The beginning of the risk leadership process is like the coming of a great storm. Clouds gather, thunder rolls, bolts of lightening crash into the parameters, yet some remain oblivious to the approaching storm of risk leadership. Management will soon learn that when the clouds of risk leadership take form, the result will inevitably be stormy weather.

The purpose of this chapter is to provide you with the four *preparation* strategies necessary for beginning the risk leadership process. As a risk agent, you must take responsibility, not just for yourself and your agency, but for every player in the organization. This involves both taking personal responsibility for your actions, as well as holding yourself accountable for the overall collective good of the organization. Once you understand the immense responsibility that comes with risk leading, you are now ready to critically and objectively assess your organization. You will need to explore the issues, people, and the overall health of your institution. This includes a detailed examination of the internal and external strengths and weaknesses, as well as threats and opportunities. Once you are focused on the true reality of the situation, you must begin the process of recruiting others to join your effort. Gaining allies in your fight for legitimacy is central to any risk leadership process. Finally, as a risk agent you will need to join others to develop an alternative agenda. You will build a vision for the future that capitalizes on the potentialities of your agency and the organization.

Strategy 1: Assuming Responsibility

The beginning stage of any risk leadership effort starts from the spark of hope that responsibility allows us to create. A recent movie, *The Shawshank Redemption,* uses the line "a little hope is a dangerous thing" to demonstrate that the human will is resilient, unless totally broken. Risk agents, feeling the creeping sensation of "status quo-itis" that takes their will away, respond with a resounding wake up call for hope. Organizational death, though common, does not have to be the necessary outcome for reaching maturity. The ability to keep some hope and spirit alive is the key to avoiding the silent undertaker - stability and efficiency.

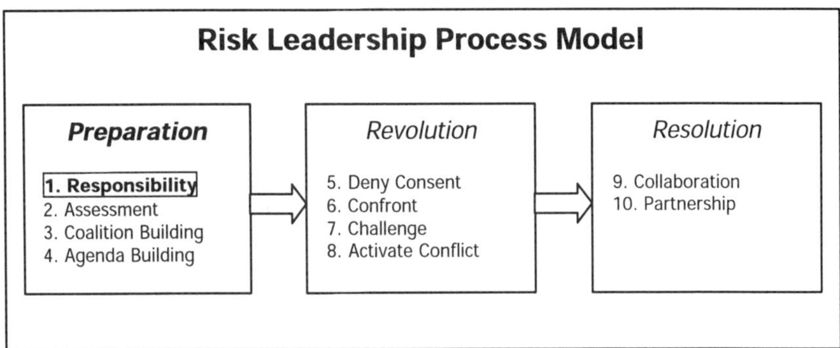

The act of responsibility, an outcome of hope, comes from two sources. The first act of responsibility is your personal investment in the action. This act of responsibility casts stability and the resulting organizational death, out of the realm of possibility and acceptability. When you take on personal responsibility, you are saying, "things matter to me." What others might overlook or take for granted, you as the risk agent do not. You take the position that many people in authority have promoted stability for too long, and thus killed a part of the organization. This personal responsibility stems from your desire to advance an issue, restructure a person, or totally reform the way business is done. True risk agents put aside their self-interests for the collective good of other organizational players. While it is unnecessarily altruistic to assert that all risk agents always put the collective good before their own, it is however, reasonable to expect that the collective good is their underlying goal in doing risk leadership. Thus, from the seeds of personal responsibility, great deeds grow.

Organizational responsibility is another critical component of the preparation stage. Organizational responsibility, or the will to act in a manner that rebuilds the organization for the good of all, is one of the most essential aspects of risk leadership. Without an accurate focus on the pulse of the organizational heart, you may well be perceived as interested in your own benefits rather than the collective will. Concern for the collective interest of the organization (or for the common good of the organization and beyond) communicates your responsibility to others in the most useful way. As long as you can effectively demonstrate your commitment to the larger organizational good, you will be perceived as credible and responsible. The essential defining element occurs when you say that it is your responsibility to make the organization better. You can no longer wait for others. When you reach this point, it is illegitimate for anyone to question your goal of improving the organization.

When you are attempting to take on responsibility you might want to consider the following tips for success:

Becoming Personally and Organizationally Responsible

- Look beyond your own condition to what really troubles the organization
- Reflect on what works and what fails in your company
- Find out what interests you and what "lights your fire"
- Realize that not all members of the organization care about what you care about
- Push yourself to make something matter to you
- Learn what the organization values
- Stand up for your organization, even when it hurts
- Take a chance on an issue to support
- Talk to others about what matters; make their concern your concern
- Find a person that you feel has the same collective good mentality and try to understand what keeps their spirit alive

Strategy 2: Assessing Your Organization

As John Gardner in his book *On Leadership* so simply stated, "the first step is not action, the first step is understanding." As with any organization worth trying to improve, risk agents must begin their journey with a desire to gain knowledge before jumping blindly into the unknown. To act before you understand is to stick your neck in the hungry lion's mouth. For those that fail to heed the warning, quick organizational execution is sure to come. Rather, risk agents should take the time and make the effort to learn about the real issues and problems before they attempt to remedy them. Physicians are held accountable with justified malpractice suits if they fail to diagnose problems, and you could face the same perilous fate.

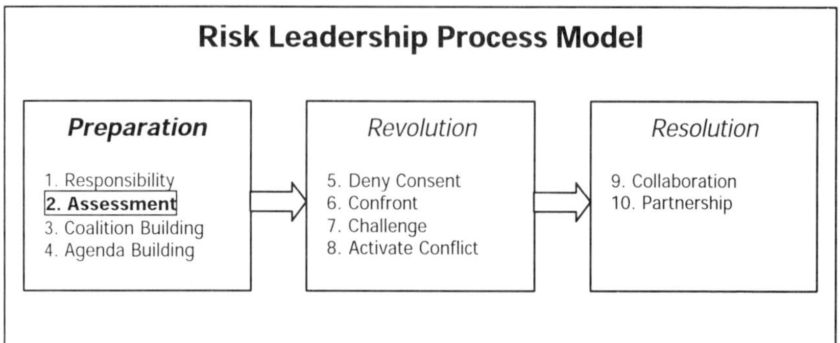

When assessing your organization, it is imperative that you understand others' thoughts on the issues, people, or the overall organizational condition. To be most effective you will need to find an issue that others can identify with, learn more about a person of concern, or recognize that there is a general sense that the organization is failing in a fundamental way. This information will be essential when you get ready to put your risk agency together.

Assessing your organization should be done by utilizing multiple methods. First, assessment requires that you study organizational members. Without understanding the people and what binds them together as a collective unit would be failure in the works. Our interest here is not to give you specific questions to ask or ways to help you poll people, rather our sole focus is to heighten your awareness of the need for individual assessment of organizational members. When you are planning your assessment there are a variety of methods you may want to choose: qualitative interviews, quantitative surveys and polls, informal conversations, and direct or indirect observations. Each of these methods has strengths and weaknesses that are well beyond the purposes of this book. Our best advice is to choose a method that is least intrusive and gives you an abundance of data from which you can draw accurate conclusions.

Another advantage of this form of assessment is that you may obtain a feel for the true pulse of the organization. Interviewing key players can give you insight on this informal culture. By understanding the organization's purpose and unwritten methods and norms, you can begin to identify the real issues of concern. Although assessing an organizational culture is extremely difficult and far from an exact science, risk agents must have some general knowledge of what makes the organization tick.

Another form of assessment involves collecting hard data on the issue, the person, or the overall organization. Here you will need to identify information concerning the internal strengths and weaknesses as well as external threats and opportunities. A tried and true "SWOT" analysis (Strengths, Weaknesses, Opportunities, and Threats) can give you vast insight into the positives and negatives of your organization. As you begin this type of assessment, it may be worthwhile to collect information about plans that have worked and missions that have failed. In addition, gathering data from outside the organization can result in an abundance of information for any risk leadership effort. For example, customers, suppliers, stockholders, and even competitors can provide invaluable knowledge that may not be available in-house.

We have a word of caution to those of you who will participate in organizational assessment. When you question others, it is always wise to avoid biasing them with your viewpoint. Get their honest opinion before you give them your side of the issue. Remember that you may even use your assessment stage as a preliminary step to recruiting those for your cause. Therefore, as you talk with others during your assessment, try to be positive and evenhanded when talking about weakness and threats. While fear may motivate you, try to keep your emotions in check and act in a responsible manner.

The basic reason for assessment is to get a realistic picture of the organization. Consider the following:

Assessing Your Organization

- Take the time you need to understand, then act on it
- Listen to what is NOT said as much as what is said
- Take all sides into account and then form your opinion
- Don't put words in people's mouths; let them own their thoughts
- Act concerned, but don't be troubled by what you see
- Talk to people you might not ordinarily talk to
- Some people may not trust you; make them more comfortable before you begin
- Don't loose your focus, but keep an open mind about the issue, person, or overall organizational malcontent
- Learn as much as possible about the culture before you leap into what troubles you
- After you have done a thorough job, collect your thoughts, form an opinion, and make some waves

Strategy 3: Building the Coalition

Risk leadership is not an individual sport; teams play this game. Putting your team together may be as easy as picking up "free agents" in the off season or "rookies" from the minor leagues. Whatever your resource for team members - finding them, recruiting them, and keeping them is essential to the process of building a risk agency. No risk agency will succeed without the support of some, and the support of many can make your effort even more productive. As a risk leader you will need to be concerned with two separate actions: recruiting new risk agents to your cause and maintaining the risk agency.

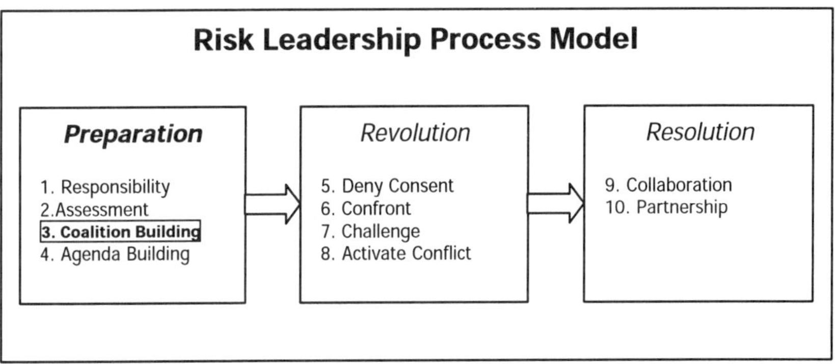

When assessing your organization you are looking at the people and their culture. It is quite common for a risk agency to be hatched during this process. Whichever assessment device is used, there is always a great deal of information that can be derived about the opinions of others in relation to the issue, person, or organizational weakness. As you interview and poll other organizational members, you will quickly recognize those players who share your common concerns about the organizational well being.

Recruitment is only a small step forward from assessing the opinions of others to the actual formation of a coalition. Once we know who is supportive, a simple informal contact is needed. This contact, like a cold sales lead, can often be difficult to initiate. Contacting some potential risk agents can be as easy as a conversation over a coffee break or an informal discussion in the hallway. Taking coworkers to lunch may also be a great place to find potential allies. During this initial contact it is important to get past ambiguity and let them know not just your position, but also the reason why you hold that position. During assessment it is important to remain removed; however, by the coalition building stage you have already determined that the issue cannot wait and that you need help to get the agency off the ground. In order to separate the critics from the true risk agents, you will need to determine the depth of their commitment. Again, this may be difficult and awkward, but it is essential to know who is really willing to confront and challenge authority.

Once you have commitments from people, the risk agency should develop a culture unique to itself. This culture, in many cases, is the tie that binds risk agents to the effort. In most cases the mutual interests will keep people motivated about the purpose of the risk agency. Maintaining this alliance is enhanced because you will likely have a "common enemy" in the issue, the person, or the organizational weakness that drives your agency. What should not happen is the "demonization" of the issue or person you have rallied against. The risk agency must stay collected and rational, even in the early and emotional stages of the revolution. Maintaining the risk agency is done through constant rekindling of the spirit that brought you together. There must be progression in your resistance movement in order to keep the momentum. Progress comes when the risk agency can chalk up wins for their effort. Even the small ones count. Winning these small battles early can reassure committed risk agents, as well as help recruit new revolutionaries.

Building a Coalition of Risk Agents

- Reach out and connect as a friend and colleague first
- Be as selective as you think you can be when recruiting
- Taking risks at this stage can "tip your hat" too much sometimes
- Identify those people who have the desire to change the world and the energy to make it happen
- Let your assessment drive you, but listen to your intuition
- Once you let them "in," trust them as an ally
- Focus your efforts on sympathetic stable guard members, external advocates, and renegade managers
- Reach basic agreement on your purpose early; iron out the specifics after you know all members are interested in the same result
- Create a subculture, or a counter-culture, of revolutionaries in which others want to participate
- Keep your agency small enough to be responsive, but large enough to show strength and get something done

Strategy Four: Forming the Alternative Agenda

Prior to the agenda building stage, you have assessed, recruited, and maintained members. During the early parts of the risk leadership process, you may have tinkered with the notion of creating a unified purpose, but the real vision work may well be done after members are on the scene. As with any organization, team, relationship, or human grouping, a mission and vision is negotiated and created through an interactive process. To say that your risk agency is unified around a particular issue, person, or organizational weakness is only a small part of the story. This serves as the "mission" of the risk agency. The mission is the *why* you and others have come together. Most people will indicate their agreement with parts or all of this stated mission, but the real work comes with the formation of the vision. The alternative agenda is the solution or "vision" which provides the direction for the risk agency. Each risk agent will likely have a different concept of what the

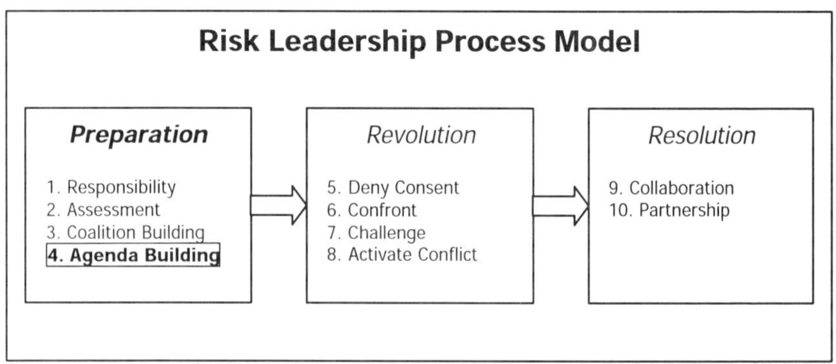

vision or solution to the problem should be. However, over a period of time the revolutionaries will need to reach an agreement on their alternative agenda.

The ability of the risk agency to make decisions is critical at this stage. Agreeing about the basic purpose and direction of the risk agency is only one step in this decision making process. Concurrently, as a member of the risk agency you will need to make multiple decisions regarding the necessary strategies for implementing the revolt. Decisions about the way that power will be denied, how confrontation will be established, the rationale given for the revolt, how conflict will be activated, and how management and the risk agency will resolve the dispute are all important decisions that will need to be addressed.

There are a variety of ways in which risk agencies make decisions. Some may try more democratic means, which may divide the team and marginalize those that are on the loosing side of the decision. Others may try to autocratically determine the fate which may run the risk of losing valuable agency members. Finally, some risk agencies may attempt to make decisions by collaborating on possible solutions and agreeing in a consensual manner. Decision through consensus is probably the least efficient and most time-consuming method possible; however, the benefits are unequaled. Benefits to consensus making include increased satisfaction among participants, enhanced commitment of the risk agents, "buy in" for the process, and improved legitimacy of the risk agency and individual agents.

Achieving consensus and creating a unified front will strengthen your risk leadership agenda. This unified front consists of both a mutual vision or direction and the strong commitment of those involved. First, a vision is crucial to let others understand your agenda. Without vision, others will fail to understand the real role of the risk agency and the planned course of action. Make your vision clear enough so that others know where you stand, while at the same, time make it inclusive enough to appeal to a larger audience. Second, you must publicly commit to your alternative agenda. Committing to a project or idea privately is one thing, coming out in the open with your judgment on an issue is quite another. If there is strength in numbers, then the risk agency's numbers must be visible. Commitment comes only after people have bought into the vision in which they have created.

When your risk agency prepares for its first encounter, the denial of power, there are a few pre-game aspects to understand. Once the agenda is formed, the vision is sold to all, and commitment is in place, you and your agency must take note of the strategic nature of the battle to come. The risk agency has an issue, person, or organization to "fix." The reality of the situation suggests that your agency needs to face the oncoming task with the composure and tact of any professional. In many ways preparing for risk leading is much like preparing for any other major organizational change. Your agency must realize that there will be bumps along the way, and that a cool head and the passion to overcome those bumps is essential for success. While emotion and feelings may well motivate or "build the fire" for your agency, you need to grasp the logical and rational side of the process in order to be successful. Consider the following tips:

Forming an Alternative Agenda

- Keep in mind that a revolution takes commitment and hard work
- Allow people to retain an identity aside from your risk agency
- Don't manage risk agents the way that top management manages them; empower them
- Be a role model for risk leading; show people that you have the ability to stand up for what you believe in
- Provide a support network for those members that you think may have trouble going through the rest of the process
- Input is crucial for the success of your agency; build in ample opportunity for people to add value to the agency
- Listen to others' visions and modify your views as necessary
- Develop clear reasons for advancing the risk agency; don't assume that everyone knows the rationale the way you do
- Understand that your agency will be stronger with more planning, thought, and perseverance. Don't leap before you look
- Work to find a consensus on both the vision and strategies for its implementation

Summary

Leading a risk agency into the process of risk leadership is not easy. It takes time, study, effort, and passion to condense the reality of a few revolutionaries into a unified state of cohesive movement. Assuming responsibility for the organization is the first step in saving it. Management may try to bridle your will, but you must fight this attempt because you envision and embrace the possibilities. In your assessment you are looking for the bravest and best, those with a little "fire in the belly." As you collect your data you are prepared to contact them and draft them into your endeavor. Risking everything, you meet and determine the vision and future of the organization.

The storm forms as risk agents and their allies combine efforts. The storm grows as the risk agency takes purpose and direction. The storm threatens as the risk agency prepares for the first attack. The storm is upon us as we risk everything in the first step of the process - denying power.

Chapter 8

Revolution: The Storm Rages

Introduction

Once the commitment to engage in risk leadership has been made, risk agents must be feverishly assessing and forming a coalition to lead the fight. These early stages of risk leadership may seem more like the "glory days" than any other time. Collecting information, developing a strong support coalition, and committing to a mission and vision are all precursors to the real risk leadership event. The next stage begins the revolutionary phase of the risk leadership process.

In the risk leadership process, the agency moves from the denial of power to confrontation, challenge, conflict, and ultimately to a collaborative end. This chapter addresses the four revolutionary strategies in the risk leadership process. Denial of power, as the initial step of the revolution, involves the risk agency standing steadfast to top management and saying "NO" to a policy, person, or overall organizational failing. In the confrontation stage, where top management takes their swipe at the risk agency, risk leaders must stand their ground in the face of attack. Next, the challenge stage encourages the risk agency to build a rational case for their position. Finally, the activation of conflict occurs when both sides understand the others' position and "dig in" for the long haul. All of these stages involve some form conflict between top management and the risk agency. In many ways these stages represent the real work of the risk agency - creating the storm that hammers away at the tired status quo techniques of top management. These strategies are the most difficult to enact, given the affliction of most people to try to avoid conflict at whatever cost. Denial of power, confrontation, challenge, and conflict put the risk agency right at the doorway of top management. They are not begging to be heard, rather demanding an audience. Our focus on these four strategies takes us to the difficult part of risk leadership - how to do it. We give specific recommendations on how to perform each of the four strategies in almost any workplace.

Strategy 5: Denying the Consent to be Governed

Denial of the consent to be governed, as the first part of the process, initiates the revolt. As we have indicated before, hesitancy in this step can hinder the entire process to the finish. The denial of consent occurs when you refuse to be subjected to the evils of the organization any longer. Something must be done, now! You, as a risk agent, must mobilize and stand tall against top management by denying the power that has always been assumed. Denial of power is not easy, especially given the fact that top management has assumed power for so long. Taking power away is tantamount to the revolt. When denying power you are essentially saying, "I will not do what you are asking." In reality, denial of power is telling top management that they can no longer push risk agents around. They must now take notice.

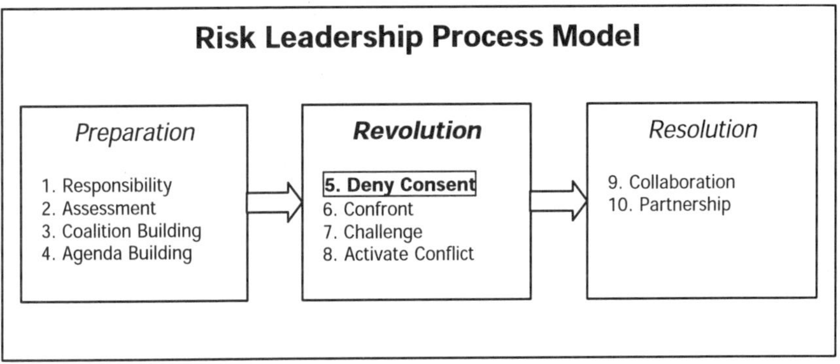

Denial of power becomes a major concern for top management because it threatens basic traditions of the organization. When the risk agency breaks these traditions, they are challenging policies, strategies, directives, and orders that management has issued. Breaking new ground, though worthwhile for organizational sanctioned events, is not appreciated in any respect if initiated by the risk agency. As top management sees it, the denial power process is seen as inciting a revolt, which is never good for business. For the risk agency, breaking ranks with top management is the first step in furthering their agenda.

Furthermore, the way that denial of power is asserted often serves as a telling tale of the risk agency's strength. One needs only to consider the impassioned students at Tienamien Square in China during the late 1980s to understand the power of denying tradition. One could just as easily consider the 1960s civil rights movement and the dramatic actions of people like King, Cleaver, and Malcolm X as further examples of challenging power. Walking arm in arm through streets filled with hateful people is a vivid metaphor for a risk agency.

One of the least intrusive means of beginning the process of risk leadership is refusing to live the organizational "line." Everyone has experienced a situation in which the organization manufactures propaganda for the sake of selling employees on an issue, person, or organizational improvement. This information, though patently false and offensive to the risk agency, is often believed by others and repeated throughout the organization. As a risk agent, you should take issue with this misinformation and act against the organizational line. Refusing to accept this line is but one small way to deny power.

Denial of power comes at a crossroads for the risk agency. Some risk agents may have the attitude that denial of power is the first step in risking the truth, their career, and their future. To publicly declare that the "emperor has no clothes" is a difficult stance to take in terms of one's future in an organization. Taking chances, like the denial of managerial power, is a step that takes the risk agency to the brink of no return. You will have a much more difficult time going "underground" after making a public declaration and denying the power of the classical and progressive leaders. However, if real change for the good of the organization is to occur, then you must take the responsibility to set aside your self-interest and stand tall in the face of management.

Denying Power

- Stand your ground; don't back down
- Deny power when it is most prudent: don't wait too long, don't jump too quick
- Stay alert to the informal network before, during, and after
- Make your stance as public as possible
- Stand up to the right person
- Pick the battle small enough to win decisively
- Don't let others dilute the intensity of the agency
- Stand guard for other risk agents as they deny power
- Keep your focus
- Understand that denial won't last forever, it may get worse before it gets better

Strategy 6: Disputing the Social Contract: Confrontation

In the confrontation stage of risk leadership, it is common for tensions to run high. Risk agents have tempted fate and stood up in an act of self-empowerment. Without exception, this act will agitate management. Few managers have the patience to allow a risk agency to "step out of line" with the company, even if the issue is trivial. This is seen as an act of treason. However, risk agents are free to act only when they are competent, interested in the collective good, and believe they are right!

In confrontation, the risk agency stands firm on their denial. The denial stage occurs out of frustration, but confrontation is more a result of persistence and determination. While denial of power provided the first shot, the confrontation stage is more like an "in the trenches" armed assault. Confrontation is more emotional than most other stages because the risk agency must now keep standing in response to the first onslaught from top management. Risk agents cry "enough is enough" and hold the line against the ill-fated advances of management.

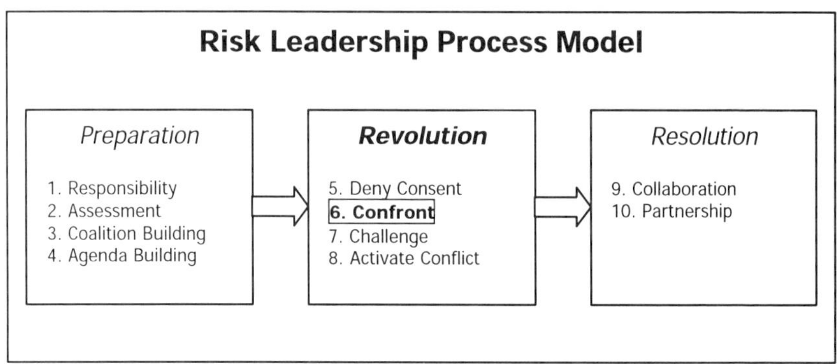

Confrontation occurs when the risk agency has made their position clear and top management has countered by reinforcing the organizational line. Management will likely be surprised by the strength and courage of the risk agency. Even though management may recognize the organizational concerns of the risk agency, they will not give in to the pressures without a fight. Management creates a situation in which the risk agency must commit to the battle. During the confrontation stage, management does a double take and says "you said what to me?" It is at this point that you must take ownership and responsibility for your denial of power. While management may think that the risk agency does not "have what it takes" to finish the battle, it is your role to prove them wrong. It is critical at this time that you prove your determination and persistence regarding your commitment to the organizational good.

When confrontation occurs it is likely that management will know that the problem is real. Furthermore, the strong showing of your risk agency in the denial and confrontational stages communicates that you and your colleagues are not going away. This message is noticed by others and is hard to minimize given the collective good focus of the risk agency. In no time you will likely gain needed supporters, due to the fact that you stood up for what they believed in and defended your position.

To facilitate your confrontation consider the following:

Confronting Management

- Remember that management acts out of anger and fear; you shouldn't
- Always keep your vision in mind
- Remind yourself that confrontation leads to change
- Keep management off balance
- Overcome obstacles when changing issues, people, or the organization
- Prepare for the challenge
- Don't flinch; no weakness allowed
- Be resolute in your mission
- Don't listen to non-players or antagonists
- Maintain your will to change with a positive, proactive agenda

Strategy 7: Challenging the System

While the denial of power and confrontation stages are quite important, risk agencies get nowhere if the challenge stage is left out of the picture. In the challenge stage, the risk agents are interested in providing a clear rationale for why they are confronting top management. The risk agency is interested in delivering good reasons for why they have spoken out about the issue, person, or the overall organizational status. Credible evidence must serve as the foundation for

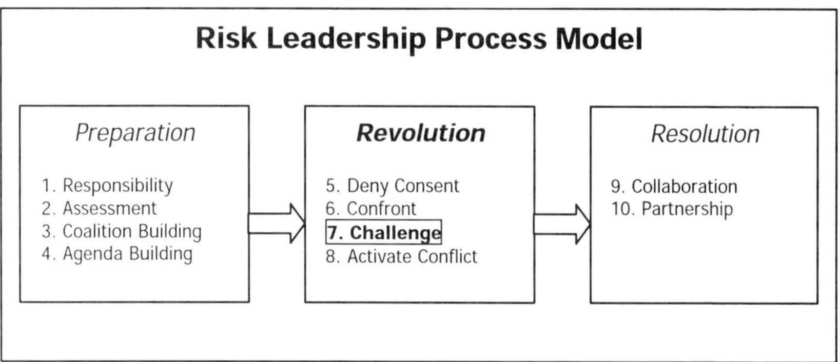

any successful challenge. As a risk agent, you need to have a clearly defined purpose for your efforts. You must provide reliable and believable evidence to support the positions your agency is taking. While evidence can often be found to support a variety of sides, you must search for incontrovertible evidence of the problems you are trying to fix. Understanding your objective and evidence is important, but being able to communicate those elements is also critical to the risk agency effort. Risk leadership may fail when others in the organization do not understand the real story behind your coalition and its purpose.

Focusing on the evidence and the agency's mission provides the background needed for people to buy into the revolution.

At this stage, your challenge should be based on ideas, not on emotion. Every good challenge must be based on rational thought and good reasons for the change. Focusing on just the emotion of change does not give you the power you will need to fight the fight. In fact, many risk agents may be minimized as "hot heads." The challenge stage is considered the "why" stage of risk leadership, given the focus on exposing good ideas and defeating bad ones.

Understanding what goes into an effective challenge is important, but it is also important to understand the different ways to challenge an issue, person, or the larger organization. Challenging management on an issue may be the easiest. Once the real issue has been identified, your risk agency needs to develop a mission to pursue. Your mission should be driven by the need to fix the issue under contention, so that your focus is very narrow and defined. Next, challenging management about a person in power is more difficult. Often the challenge is more emotional and personal than it should be. Separating the person from their troublesome behaviors is hard to do, but your agency must find a way to depersonalize the challenge. To launch a successful challenge in this situation, you must develop alternative solutions to the person in question. Often this can be solved if the person is reassigned or additional training occurs. Finally, when addressing widespread organizational problems, you will need to focus your energies on changing the overall organizational structure and culture. As a result, this form of challenge is the most complex and troublesome. Issue centered challenge focuses on one issue, whereas changing the entire organization takes a much wider view. Focusing on the general malaise is not enough. Your agency will need to target its efforts on more specific elements to change. Furthermore, given the larger arena, the need for evidence becomes even greater. Whether challenging an issue, person, or the entire organization, your risk agency efforts must be built on a solid foundation of realistic and rational arguments.

Challenging management is not easy work. It takes purpose and proof. As you consider the best ways you can challenge, you might be able to adapt some of the following suggestions to your organization:

Challenging the System

- Focus on the purpose first
- Make your point as simple as possible for all to understand
- Stand behind your claim
- "Research" your evidence
- Control your emotion by focusing on the facts
- Keep management on the defensive; they'll be more likely to cave in
- Make sure to give management a way out of the problem
- You will have to argue your point; be prepared
- Get support from your agency when you make the case
- Don't quibble over the irrelevant, but fight for the points that matter to your agency

Strategy 8: Activating Conflict

It is common for risk agents to move past challenge right into argumentation and conflict. In fact, the challenge stage involves the conflict of ideas. Most people are taught that conflict is a dangerous thing and that it should be avoided if at all possible. One point about risk leadership is clear - real change comes only when management's ideas have been challenged on a rational basis. Only through extensive argumentation and the conflict of ideas, can real change take hold in a landscape that is littered with stability and false change prophets. Protracted conflict over ideas is necessary to make the point stick to management and the organization. One of the credos of risk leadership is that out of dissensus comes consensus. Out of conflict comes agreement and collaboration.

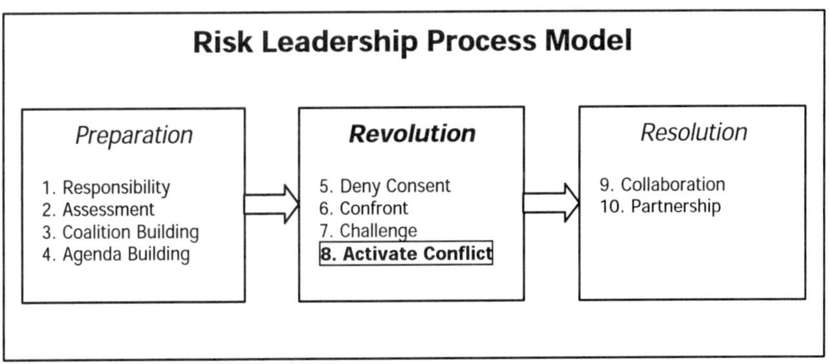

Permanent attention comes from the ability to highlight the real differences between management and the risk agency. Challenge and conflict are ideally suited to give serious attention to the risk agency and its issue, person, or organizational problem. Risk agents make their big splash by standing up for what they think is right. Conflict is the stage during which risk agents go beyond standing their ground, and actually begin to implement their agenda despite the views of management. Conflict is more than just standing up and speaking out for what is right; conflict is about doing the risk agenda while others sort it out.

Now that your risk agency is noticed, you have the power to sell the collective good agenda to a wide array of other organizational members. This is absolutely necessary for change. It will take the support of many others, both in and outside of the organization, in order to implement your agency's alternative agenda. In earlier times, top management could have ignored the will of its organizational members, but with improved information technology and rising expectations, this is not realistic. When subjected to the scrutiny of the total organization, management must consider and reconsider their position. This conflict stage, therefore, allows the risk agency to highlight their position and take it to those that benefit from it most - the larger organizational community.

During this conflict stage, your risk agency must continue to work toward implementing its alternative agenda. Work cannot stop just because management does not immediately convert to your position; in fact, this will rarely happen. It will take hard work and effort to change management and your risk agency must show results in order to be perceived as legitimate and credible. Even small steps towards implementing the risk agenda can provide momentum.

A final consideration for the risk agency should be damage control. Often times conflict can turn ugly. Even though the risk agency may have the right and the power, they may not be truly appreciated.

In this case, they need to turn their attention to damage control. Damage control consists of a grassroots effort to rebuild support. Risk agency members may be considered the "rebels" and be somewhat outcast. As risk efforts move forward, the agency needs to find a way to gather the support of those that may not understand the real benefits that the revolution provides. In essence, damage control is the regrouping of your risk agency after a particularly difficult confrontation and challenge.

The following includes helpful suggestions to consider as you activate conflict:

Activating Conflict

- Act out your agenda
- Try to keep conflict productive; stay on the issues
- Maintain espirit de corps by supporting others in your risk agency
- Focus on the solution, not on the past
- Talk to organizational members that may not understand your agency
- Be prepared for quick change; collaboration may come soon
- Conflict may require rattling sabres, don't get your feelings hurt
- Consistently backup what you have to say with credibility
- Stay in the forefront on your issue, don't let management grandstand
- You can still fail at this, so be humble and focus on the common good

Summary

Some may argue that these four strategies are too oriented toward erupting conflict on the stable organizational landscape. They are right. However, without denial of power, confrontation, challenge, and conflict there will be no long-term change, only incremental death. When we deny power, we are refusing to follow management's path to organizational destruction. When we confront, we are digging in and telling the authority establishment that we are serious and we will not go away. When we are challenging, we are challenging the ideas behind the issue, people, or organizational weaknesses. It is important to remember that this challenge stage is based on rational facts and data, not on emotional appeals. Finally when we are initiating conflict, we are participating in a protracted debate with management. During this conflict stage, we are not waiting for others to begin to implement our alternative agenda.

These important stages of the risk leadership process may take some risk agencies days, others months, and in some cases even years to complete. Ultimately if you want to shake things up, you will need to keep confronting and challenging the status quo. Absent a real reason to change, management will not make the substantial changes necessary for organizational survival. Thus, the risk agency must stay at the forefront of the key issues and define the path for the rest of the organization.

These revolutionary strategies will bring you closer to true self-empowerment. Given the fact that classical and progressive leaders have not delivered on their promises of shared power, the risk agency must take it upon themselves. You have much to gain and only dissatisfaction to loose. You should not wait any longer to take up the fight for self-empowerment. These four stages represent the only way to liberate both your agency and yourself. As we have said before, the real risk is not doing risk leadership.

Chapter 9

Resolution: Clearing Skies

Introduction

The final phase of the risk leadership process explains how the risk agency and top management reach their objectives and how they develop a long-term profitable relationship and culture. Risk leadership is an approach inspired by and arrived at through conflict in several different forms. A risk agency must deny power, confront management, challenge ideas, and finally engage in protracted conflict with management. In addition, risk agents take on their charge based on the fallible nature of the organization, a person that thwarts change, or an important issue that defies resolution through normal channels. Risk agents walk through fire to achieve their objective - working together out of mutual respect and trust to resolve the issue, reform the person, or revise the general organizational problem.

In this model, risk leaders will ultimately recognize the need to collaborate with management. Thinking that risk agents are simply interested in conflict is shortsighted. In reality, conflict is merely the method used to reach collaboration. The final step in concluding the risk leadership endeavor includes both collaboration and the creation of a unique partnership between the combative parties. If risk leaders only make it to the conflict stage and then terminate their movement, they have failed in achieving their ultimate outcome. Reaching the collaboration and partnership stage ensures that the risk agency does not have to resort to the earlier stages of the revolutionary battle every time change is necessary. When management recognizes that the risk agency is a valuable contributor to the organization, then the risk leadership effort has been a success. This chapter addresses this final phase of the risk leadership process - collaboration and the development of an uncomfortable partnership.

Strategy 9: Conflict to Collaboration

Collaboration, as the initial stage in the resolution process, is probably the most difficult to achieve. Reaching collaboration is difficult for two reasons. First, it is hard for many risk agents to see past their opposition with management. It is realistic to assume that some risk agents may get bogged down in the processes of denial of power, confrontation, challenge, or even the conflict stage. This occurs when the issue becomes so impassioned that key players on both sides are unable to see the benefits of the other. As a result, both sides are not in the mood to find common ground.

A second reason that collaboration is hard to reach occurs when risk agents loose their enthusiasm for the revolution. Instead of fighting the battle to the end, they stop short. This can happen for many different reasons. Perhaps individual risk agents tire and resort to more comfortable surroundings. Furthermore, internal disagreement within the agency on its overall purpose and vision could also lessen the will to fight. It may also happen when the risk agency takes the easy way out and decides to compromise away their position before they even attempt to collaborate. Whatever the case, risk agencies may not always be able to successfully make it through all of the stages. Therefore, risk agents need to be cautious about their role in the transition to collaboration. Given these possibilities, only the strong and most determined risk agencies will succeed in reaching resolution.

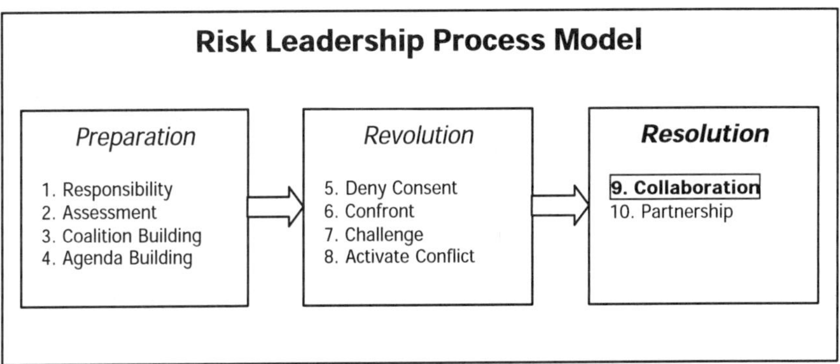

One of the biggest mistakes a risk agency can make is to stop the risk leadership process before they reach the collaboration stage. The key to a successful collaboration process involves the ability to move past the easier compromise option. This failure happens for all the wrong reasons, namely, the fear of conflict and the desire to "get it over with." The primary difference between compromise and collaboration is the way the risk agency is treated. Under compromise, the risk agency is still subservient to the demands of management. Compromise occurs because the risk agency fears continuing the process. The risk agency looses all the ground they have won because there is no mutual respect.

On the other hand, during collaboration the risk agency is treated with more respect and is not forced to sell out their basic principles.

The collaboration stage should be marked by finding the best solution for addressing the issue, personnel concern, or organizational illness that started the entire process. The solution should place both parties in a situation where they mutually rely on one another to implement the change. The risk agency needs the resources of top management to make the change happen. Whereas, management needs the competency of risk agency members to make the implementation successful. Together, they must collaborate in order to make the solution happen. If one party controls the solution, then mistrust is a likely result and the risk agency and top management will find themselves back in the revolutionary stages. This process of exchange, where both parties have mutual respect and trust for one another, is crucial in order to have a real chance at collaboration.

During collaboration both parties must come to the implicit agreement that the other party adds value to the organization. This will be more difficult for management because they believe that they should have uncontested control of the organization. This is equally difficult for the risk agency because they believe their mission better serves the collective good. Both parties are partially right and partially wrong. The fact is that both stand to gain much more if they form a cooperative bond that maximizes their unique talents and bridges the gap that conflict has created. This cooperative bond can only happen if both parties recognize what the other brings to the table. Essentially, both parties exchange mutual respect, admitting that the other adds value to the company. They must also recognize that lasting change will occur only when they work together for the collective good. As a risk leader, you must realize that management has legitimate authority to make decisions. Management must also realize that without key personnel that support their decisions, they may as well talk to themselves. Working together means looking past weaknesses and capitalizing on the unique strengths the other party brings with them.

As part of the collaboration stage, management has to give the risk agency credit for the agenda they have proposed. They must be able to admit that the alternative agenda adds value to the company. When management is ready to say that risk leaders have advanced the collective good of the organization, they legitimize the power and actions of the risk agency and liberate the entire movement. Without acknowledgment of the battle fought, the warriors will harbor tension and anger and feel that they have been overlooked in organizational rebuilding.

Now you are ready for collaboration! Understanding the extreme difficulties in pursuing resolution, you might keep the following suggestions in mind as your agency works toward collaboration:

Successful Collaboration

- Now, more than ever, focus on your objective
- Focus on what the other side has to offer
- Remain cognizant of compromise strategies
- Try to mentally put away conflict
- Visualize success and sell other risk agents on the rewards of working together at this stage
- Remember, you are at the end of the process; don't make critical mistakes that cost you all the gains you've made
- Stay in close contact with others - both risk agents and management
- Be aware of the implications of what you are offering, don't sell out
- Be mission and vision centered
- Show that you are reasonable, but very convicted about your beliefs

Strategy 10: Creating an Uncomfortable Partnership

The final stage of the risk leadership paradigm is the creation of a permanent culture or partnership that overcomes the biases and self-interests of the prior regime. Clearly, there will be a major change in the organizational landscape after top management and risk agents have experienced this process. At this point, risk agents can be called true risk leaders since they have accomplished their objective through means that were, in retrospect, quite difficult. They have overcome the severest of obstacles and have made things happen in their organization, while their colleagues merely waited for organizational death. They arrive at the bargaining table as a true vested partner in the power structure of the organization. As risk leaders, they act as a representative for one side of the uncomfortable partnership, insuring future success of the total organization.

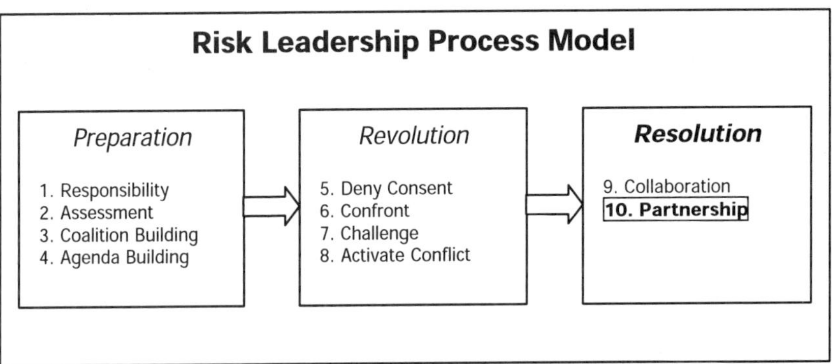

The uncomfortable partnership is the final step toward realizing the ultimate goal of the risk agency - the ability to empower all and transform the organization for the collective good. For many organizations, the risk leadership process will require a long-term cultural adjustment. Risk leadership is not a quick fix that allows people to just walk in, apply the theory, walk out two days later, and expect it to work. It will fail! Protracted cultural transformation is more likely to alter the organization than a quick two-day approach to change. Therefore, the basic charge of the risk leader is to create a long-term sustained threat to the power structure. This legitimate threat allows people to have more say over their destiny - to empower the masses on an issue, a person, or the overall organizational health.

The uncomfortable partnership also gives the risk agency some guarantees as they face the "new" organization. Players come and go from the organizational scene, but the risk agency does not want to loose the ground they have achieved. Therefore, they must create a long-term partnership which recognizes the threat of further risk leadership endeavors. The risk leadership game must continue despite the fact that some members of the risk agency may move on or get promoted.

Risk leaders and management must have a shared interest in avoiding continuous conflict. Collaboration is a great attempt in reaching mutual interest. However, collaboration alone is not enough to guarantee that peace will last. Rather it will take the fullest commitment of all parties to form and maintain a partnership that seeks the collective good. Just as the risk agents have a genuine need to follow the path of conflict to improve the organization, at the end of the process they have much reason to hold their gains by collaborating in an atmosphere where there is mutual respect.

There are many demands placed on risk agents in this final phase of the process. Initially, they must begin to collaborate with their sworn enemy in the fight for the collective improvement of the organization. The risk agency must also accept the responsibility of leading the organization. This means that risk agents must accept responsibility and accountability for decision and implementation making. The risk agency must also demand some sort of verification that management is truly committed to the collective good and the empowerment of others throughout the organization. The risk agency may justifiably feel that management has to prove their commitment since they have already proven their value through the process of denial of power, confrontation, challenge, conflict, and collaboration.

Likewise, top managers also have demands placed on them in order for the "new" organization to be effective. Management must find a way to recognize the value of collaborating with employees that may not be vested in stocks and securities, but nevertheless are vested in the company. One of the most difficult things for management to realize is that people at all levels are valuable to the organization and are interested in the overall collective good of its mission. Management must also be accountable and responsible for the changes that face the organization. Management needs to understand that change is inevitable and that their concept of a stable unchanging workplace is an antiquated idea. Now that a risk agency has paved the way, top management must accept that change may occur at a faster rate, making stability an illusion.

One of the most important implications of this stage is that risk agents must be able to "flex their muscle" when addressing organizational problems. Ongoing reinforcement and a reminder of the strength and success of the risk agency are very important since people do come and go and management may overlook their improvements. Furthermore, the ability to recreate the spirit that launched the risk agency serves as a reminder to its members that they still have what it takes. Muscle flexing can also be a benefit because it illustrates to others throughout the organization that the company is alive and adaptable to change. The bottom line is that from time to time the risk agency will likely need to utilize its power to remain an active player in the partnership.

The uncomfortable partnership places both sides in check. Both the risk agency and management are now responsible not just to their own constituency, but are also accountable to all organizational players. The partnership places both parties on a more equitable playing field so that they may have more information about the other for the express purpose of making a better organization, solving an issue, or dealing with specific personnel. With both sides in check, the other does not have an advantage in dominating the game. If management has accountability and responsibility programmed into the system, why would they feel the need to fight the risk agency? Equally, if the risk agency holds management responsible and accountable, then why would they work to crush them? Neither side gets any real gain in rekindling the conflict stages of risk leadership, unless some unforeseen event precipitates it. The ability to keep the other side in check and to hold them accountable is exhausting work, but both sides have a real interest in moving past the conflict stages to mutual respect. An important element of respect for the risk organization is the ability to be accountable to your partner. Thus, culminated risk leadership is the creation of a balance power in the organization.

A final implication that emerges from this stage concerns the future direction of the company. Some top managers may feel the need to "give in" on the issue the risk agency has fought for just to control the rest of the organization. However, this approach is shortsighted. The uncomfortable partnership will likely consist of occasional fights over access and control in the agenda of the organization. Management is best served by allowing the risk agency input into the driving vision of the organization. The risk agency must grasp the opportunity but be respectful of the awesome power of charting a course for the future. Both sides have an interest in making sure that the other is an active participant, but together they must aspire for greater heights than the organization was able to reach before.

The risk agency and top management have a great deal of work in the uncomfortable partnership stage. Even after all the conflict, the fighting, and shifting control of the company, both sides must come back to the table in an effort to address the many issues of concern. They must find a way to work together to make the organization better after they solve the issues, tackle the personnel problems, and stem the organizational distress call.

In an effort to help you develop this important partnership with management, we have provided you with the following suggestions and warnings:

Creating the Uncomfortable Partnership

- Resist compromise and work hard for collaboration
- Institutionalize the risk leadership approach
- Start from points of agreement and then work into points of disagreement
- Make associations with management that will help the risk agency
- Don't sell out your own mission
- Be open-minded as far as the common good of the organization is concerned
- Keep the battles fresh in mind, but learn how to forgive others
- Make it a point to keep other risk agents informed
- When you feel that management wants to stray, call them on it
- Remember that change is hard work and it may take time to institutionalize all the changes you have made
- Be forward focused, remember the past, and stay acutely aware of the present

Summary

As the risk agency members move into the final two stages of the risk leadership process, they are more concerned with the capacity to move ahead rather than with the need to engage in conflict. Though conflict and dissensus are necessary elements of risk leadership, at some point the risk agency and top management have a mutual interest in getting beyond disagreement and into a collaborative arrangement. Be aware that the resolution stage of risk leadership can easily fall back into the confrontational mode. Therefore, the risk agency and management must constantly strive for common ground on the important issues facing the organization. An early return to more conflict can only damage both parties and the overall health of the company. Collaboration is probably the most difficult stage to achieve; however, the uncomfortable partnership stage is likely to be the most difficult to maintain. Making long-range plans based on trust may be one of the most difficult tasks that risk leaders and management can undertake together.

Central to the entire risk process is the ultimate objective that the risk agency strives for - legitimacy, power, and most importantly, self-empowerment. Risk leadership, in these final stages, is and should be characterized by an increase in true empowerment which benefits the collective good of the entire organization. While issues are solved, personnel is reorganized, and the organization is improved, the real long-term measure of success for the risk agents is their ability to empower themselves.

Chapter 10

Assessing Your Risk Leadership Skills

Introduction

Risk leadership is serious business. You are not just putting your organizational life on the line, but the lives of other people in your agency as well. As such you need to understand exactly where you stand as a risk agent when preparing to move into risk leadership encounters. In order to fully understand your interest and ability to participate in risk leadership, it is necessary to complete the behavioral survey - *Risk Leadership Inventory.* Understanding your overall risk leadership aptitude is important, but you must also learn how well you are equipped to start the preparation stage. You need to know how willing and able you are to actually conduct the revolution. You will also need to be knowledgeable about your ability to overcome conflict and collaborate in the resolution stage. Finally, it will be helpful to assess your own personal ability to perform the 10 specific risk leadership strategies. The *Risk Leadership Inventory* measures each of these elements, as well as your overall risk leadership effectiveness.

This chapter assists you in learning more about your individual abilities and attitudes relating to risk leadership. You are asked to complete the *Risk Leadership Inventory* and score it on the appropriate form included in this chapter. You will learn more about what your score means and learn how to interpret those scores for each of the stages of risk leadership. After you finish your self-assessment, you will know much more about your abilities as a potential risk leader. Specifically, you should have a much better understanding of your ability to prepare for a risk leadership effort, conduct an actual risk leadership revolution, and finally, effectively resolve the issues that have hindered your organization. Understanding your abilities is the first step in the process of becoming a successful risk leader. Furthermore, once you learn about your abilities, you will be better equipped to help others contribute to your risk leadership effort.

Rationale

As we have mentioned in earlier chapters, doing risk leadership is not simple and probably not natural for most. Some risk agents will have to work harder at it than others. It is also likely that some people may not have the desire to move in that direction due to their fears or the security of the status quo. It is our premise that the organization of the future will demand risk leadership. The changing organizational structure will call for very robust changes in the way that people lead. It is our feeling that risk leadership will be necessary as organizations are forced to change and adapt.

Understanding your ability as a potential risk leader is critically important for a successful risk leadership effort. Given the real possibility that not everyone is a "natural" risk leader, there is a great need to understand your ability as it relates to preparation, revolution, and resolution. After you have a better understanding of your score, you can invest more time working on areas where you feel that your skills may need improvement. Obviously, learning more about your skills now will assist you as you begin your own risk leadership effort.

Risk Leadership Inventory

The *Risk Leadership Inventory* is a self-reporting assessment instrument designed to measure your practice of risk leadership. The following 30 statements assess the extent to which you actually engage in risk leadership behaviors. Read each statement carefully, then determine the choice that best corresponds with your actual behavior.

You have 5 choices:

1 = Rarely

2 = Once in a While

3 = Sometimes

4 = Fairly Often

5 = Almost Always

Record your responses in the space provided:

1= Rarely 2=Once in a While 3=Sometimes 4=Fairly Often 5=Almost Always

_____ 1. I assume personal responsibility for the success of my organization.

_____ 2. I encourage and participate in teamwork with those who share similar beliefs.

_____ 3. My arguments with management are based on facts and evidence.

_____ 4. Despite disagreement, I am willing to work with management for the good of the organization.

_____ 5. I am willing to both challenge and collaborate with management in an uncomfortable partnership.

_____ 6. Organizational improvement is my responsibility.

_____ 7. Using a rational argument, I openly challenge the policies of management.

_____ 8. I refuse to change my position even after management's angry reaction to my challenge.

_____ 9. I stand my ground even when management threatens punishment.

_____ 10. I stand up to management when they are wrong.

_____ 11. I assume personal responsibility for my work assignment.

_____ 12. I actively seek out and join others who share the same concerns about the organization.

_____ 13. Even when management re-exerts their power, I refuse to bend.

_____ 14. My allies and I are unified in our concern for the collective good of the organization.

_____ 15. I am not afraid to present an alternative agenda to management's policies.

1= Rarely 2=Once in a While 3=Sometimes 4=Fairly Often 5=Almost Always

______ 16. I recognize the limitations and competencies of upper management.

______ 17. I actively seek consensus with my organizational allies.

______ 18. I demand that management accepts the legitimacy of our right to confront and challenge them.

______ 19. I recognize my strengths and weaknesses as an effective organizational player.

______ 20. I am willing to engage in a long-term conflict with management.

______ 21. When I believe my stance is justified, I stand my ground.

______ 22. I am prepared to fight management because my position is right.

______ 23. I have a good understanding of the strengths and weaknesses of my organization.

______ 24. I am willing to risk conflict with management for the purpose of making our organization better.

______ 25. Even after extended conflict, I appreciate management's value to the organization.

______ 26. I join others to create an alternative agenda for organizational success.

______ 27. I am willing to work with management to establish a common vision and purpose for the organization.

______ 28. I deny management's ability to exercise their power when their policies hurt the organization.

______ 29. I am willing to continually engage in confrontational strategies to make the organization better.

______ 30. I recruit others both inside and outside the organization to serve as allies.

Scoring Your Risk Leadership Inventory

Your *Risk Leadership Inventory* is scored in three different ways. First, your total score reflects your overall level of participation in risk leadership. Second, your scores on selected questions will be used to determine your participation in the three risk leadership processes (preparation, revolution, and resolution). Finally, your scores on selected questions will be used to determine your participation in the 10 risk leadership strategies. To compute your level of risk leadership complete the following:

Total Risk Leadership Inventory Score

Add your scores for all 30 statements.

Insert that number in the box..............................

This is your total Risk Leadership score.

To understand your level of preparation, revolution, and resolution:

Risk Leadership Inventory Subscales

Add your scores for statements. (1,2,6,11,12,14,16,17,19,23,26,30)

Insert that number in the box..............................

This is your score for **preparedness** as it relates to Risk Leadership.

****

Add your scores for statements. (3,7,8,9,10,13,15,20,21,22,24,28)

Insert that number in the box..............................

This is your score for **revolution** as it relates to Risk Leadership.

****

Add your scores for statements. (4,5,18,25,27,29)

Insert that number in the box..............................

This is your score for **resolution** as it relates to Risk Leadership.

To understand your rating for each of the 10 strategies of risk leadership, complete the following:

Risk Leadership Strategies

Add your scores for statements. (1, 6, 11)
Insert that number in the box..............................
This is your score for **assuming responsibility** as it relates to Risk Leadership.

****

Add your scores for statements. (16, 19, 23)
Insert that number in the box..............................
This is your score for **assessment** as it relates to Risk Leadership.

****

Add your scores for statements. (2, 12, 30)
Insert that number in the box..............................
This is your score for **building coalitions** as it relates to Risk Leadership.

****

Add your scores for statements. (14, 17, 26)
Insert that number in the box..............................
This is your score for **forming an agenda** as it relates to Risk Leadership.

****

Add your scores for statements. (10, 21, 28)
Insert that number in the box..............................
This is your score for **denying power** as it relates to Risk Leadership.

****

Add your scores for statements. (8, 9, 13)
Insert that number in the box..............................
This is your score for **confrontation** as it relates to Risk Leadership.

****

Add your scores for statements. (3, 7, 15)
Insert that number in the box..............................
This is your score for **challenging the system** as it relates to Risk Leadership.

Risk Leadership Strategies, cont.

Add your scores for statements. (20, 22, 24)

Insert that number in the box..............................

This is your score for **activating conflict** as it relates to Risk Leadership.

****

Add your scores for statements. (4, 25, 27)

Insert that number in the box..............................

This is your score for **collaborating** as it relates to Risk Leadership.

****

Add your scores for statements. (5, 18, 29)

Insert that number in the box..............................

This is your score for **creating an uncomfortable partnership** as it relates to Risk Leadership.

Interpreting Your Risk Leadership Inventory

Before you can actually interpret your risk leadership scores, it is important to note a few things. While the *Risk Leadership Inventory* has been tested successfully on many different populations, each person has an individual response. Simply put, there is a high likelihood that your scores on risk leadership and the sub-processes are reflective, and perhaps even predictive of your risk leadership behaviors. However, there will likely be special circumstances where you may exceed or fall short of expectations. Keep in mind that these scores are general reflections of your risk leadership ability and should be interpreted as such.

The first score you should examine is your *total risk leadership score.* As you view your score, keep in mind that scores of 120 or above suggest that you fairly often or very often engage in risk leadership behaviors. Scores of 60 or below indicate that you engage in risk leadership only once in a while, if at all. A typical score for risk leadership ranges from 60 to 120. This indicates that you sometimes engage in risk leadership, but it is probably more situationally determined rather than a strong behavioral trait.

As you examine your *preparation subscore,* please note that a score of 48 or more indicates that you frequently engage in those behaviors which prepare you to create a risk agency. Scores of 24 or less indicate that you rarely engage in behaviors that prepare you for risk leadership. Scores ranging from 24 to 48 suggest that you are somewhat prepared to engage in risk leadership. Again, your preparation score is probably situational.

As you examine your *revolution subscore,* please note that a score of 48 or more reflects that you often deny power, confront and challenge authority, and engage in conflict. A score of 24 or less indicates that you rarely engage in revolutionary behaviors. A score ranging from 24 to 48 indicates that sometimes you participate in revolutionary behaviors.

As you examine your *resolution subscore,* please note that a score of 24 or more suggests that you are capable of collaborating and creating uncomfortable partnerships. A score of 12 or less indicates that you are unlikely to engage in behaviors that focus on collaboration and partnership building. Scores ranging from 12 to 24 suggest that at times you do participate in collaborative behaviors.

Finally, examine your *scores for each of the 10 strategies of risk leadership*. On each subscore, a score of 12 or above indicates that you fairly often to very often engage in those behaviors. A score of 6 or less indicates that you rarely or never perform those behaviors. Scores that fall in the range of 6 to 12 suggest that you sometimes engage in the behaviors for that subscale based on the needs of the situation.

Summary

Understanding the process of risk leadership is an important step toward gaining true bottom-up organizational empowerment. Part of your journey toward preparing, revolting, and resolving is understanding your abilities in each of those categories. As you interpret your scores, keep in mind that risk leadership is probably more challenging than the statements this book may reflect. Actual confrontation will be much more emotionally charged than we can ever simulate in words.

Furthermore, as you learn more about yourself in relation to your total score, your preparation, revolution, and resolution subscores, and your individual strategy subscores, you will learn what areas need to improve. This assessment should be an indicator of your ability. You should use this assessment as a diagnostic tool to understand what your abilities are and then to correct those areas that you deem improvable. Obviously, the skills at which you scored higher reflect a greater likelihood of success. In those areas where you fall short, you will want to learn more about how to better prepare yourself. Your ability to succeed as a risk leader is limited only to the extent which you attempt to improve upon your risk leadership skills.

Assessment and interpretation are important steps in your success as a risk leader. As you gain understanding, you will be much more able to fight the fight in your organization. It has been said that being blind to your strengths and weaknesses is much like playing Russian roulette. You don't know which skill is loaded and which one is not, and sometimes you do not find out until it is too late. Self-assessment of your skills is one way to minimize the risks of risk leadership, and ultimately, to help you prepare, revolt, and resolve problems in your organization.

RISK LEADERSHIP: THE MANDATE IS CLEAR

This concluding section describes the implications for risk leadership and the potential risks faced by all organizational players. In addition, the authors call upon low and mid-level employees to accept full responsibility for the success of their organizations.

Chapter 11

Implications for Risk Leadership

Introduction

As with any new idea, there are important questions about how risk leadership will effect your organization. What are the lessons we can learn from risk leadership? What are the implications for the future? What are the keys for developing a successful risk leadership culture? These are but a few concerns that need to be addressed for those who participate, or will likely participate, in risk leadership. With this chapter, we hope to not only answer some of these questions, but also give you a list of recommendations for putting risk leadership into action.

First, we provide ten "keys to success" for the risk agency. These recommendations include: when risk agents should back down; the mobilization of the risk agency; the importance of balance when risk agents are challenging and confronting management; good timing and a clear purpose; broad-based involvement and support; serving the collective good; that the reason for the revolt (change) must be based on true facts and reality; obtaining and maintaining a unified coalition; being able to overcome obstacles and sustain movement; and the importance of risk agents continuing to be productive employees.

Second, we provide eight "keys to success" for upper level management and other organizational players who observe and participate in this confrontational leadership approach. These recommendations include: the willingness of management to accept a new shared power culture and structure; the importance of healing before collaboration; recognizing the positive role and value that the risk agency brings the organization; believing that management should be rewarding rather than punishing risk takers; acknowledging that a partnership built on confrontation can be healthy for an organization; management's recognition that real and deep change is needed; encouraging the move from self-interest and power to broader organizational concerns; and finally, management's need to focus on the company's business.

While these lists of recommendations for both risk agents and top managers are not exhaustive, they do illustrate the complexities of this approach. In addition, they provide several important points that both sides must consider if the organization is going to be successful.

Keys to Success: Implications for Risk Agents

Backing down to fight another day. "There are some hills worth fighting for, and some hills worth dying for." Risk agents need the wisdom to know when to back down and retreat in their struggle with management. When the issues do not warrant a full and protracted struggle or when it becomes clear that no progress can be made using a particular strategy, the risk agency must choose to back down. Continuous confrontation without the hope of a positive outcome could even destroy the organization. The wise choice in these situations may be to retreat in an effort to save and protect the risk agency. By pursuing this approach, the risk agency can regain its momentum and energy, consolidate resources, build unity, and look for better timing or a different strategy.

Mobilization of the risk agency will vary from time to time, or from situation to situation. No organization can withstand non-stop, continuous revolution without inevitably being destroyed from within. Chaos can only take the organization so far. An effective risk leadership culture must include breathing space and time for healing to rebuild relationships. As in most change processes, an inevitable cycle also appears in the revolutionary process - confrontation is followed by a rest period and then confrontation returns again. This allows the organization to expend energy and then rejuvenate. Risk agents need to recognize when to revolt and when not to. "Pick the battles small enough to win, or big enough to matter." Risk agents need the wisdom to recognize when the issue and situation is right and when the agency has developed the power needed to sustain the process and their objective.

Activating confrontation is a balancing act. Risk agents who activate conflict and then seek collaboration must recognize that they are playing a very difficult balancing act. On one side, they are challenging management and even encouraging confrontation in the hopes of getting management's attention. On the other, they want to eventually find middle ground, negotiate, and even collaborate with those same individuals. Therefore, risk agents must challenge to get management's attention, yet not initiate so much conflict that collaboration cannot be built out of the rubble. If a collaborative relationship cannot be rebuilt, the chances for a successful transformation are slim. This unique balancing act is clearly an art and not a science. The issue or issues, the people involved, and the timing are all important elements to be considered when weighing this process. Awareness of the needs and recognition of the uniqueness of each party is also important.

Good timing and a clear purpose. For the risk agency to be successful it must recognize and act when the timing is right. This usually means that risk agents will need to mobilize against management when there is a clear threat to the organization or when there is a unique opportunity in the marketplace. Risk agents can often gain momentum when there is a sense of urgency. A clear need or purpose provides the risk agency with a better opportunity to recruit members and allies, as well as provide a better lobbying position with upper management. It is also important for risk leaders to understand that they will need to clearly explain their reasons for change to the entire organization. Success is more likely to be achieved if those throughout the organization understand why the issue is important.

Broad-based involvement and support for the risk agency. The risk agency will gain important strength if it can find supporters and allies from all corners of the company. Management is more likely to take notice when risk agency members are identified as key players throughout the organizational structure. This makes it extremely difficult for management to isolate and destroy the "trouble makers." Addressing risk agents from one or two departments is one thing, negotiating with risk agents scattered throughout the organization is clearly another. In addition, having broad-based involvement and support brings important and crucial information, expertise, talents, and required resources to the risk agency. This in turn allows the risk agency to construct their alternative agenda.

Driven to serve the collective good. The overall purpose of the risk agency must be to improve the organization and not just the agency. Risk leadership calls for risk agents to move from self-interest to the broader concerns of the collective good. This underlining principle is what gives the risk agency real power. It puts the risk agency on "high ground" as they face off with management. If the risk agency begins to serve itself at the cost of other organizational players, they will lose their noble cause and in turn lose strength and power. Operating from this basic principle, risk agency members are in a better position to recruit, motivate, and unify others as they actively engage top management. This also puts management in a difficult position; how can they destroy their own employees when they have the health of the organization at heart?

The reason for the change must be based on true facts. Revolution for the sake of revolution will not serve risk agents, top managers, or the organization itself. Risk leadership must be based on well-founded organizational issues, the lack of effective leadership, or the need for transformation. Before action is taken, risk agents must research and truly understand the complexities behind the issues. If the proposed change is not based on reality (actual conditions in the environment), management will quickly exploit and defeat the risk agency. Therefore, it is imperative that risk leaders make their agenda decisions based on accurate information and data if they hope to successfully serve the organization and accomplish their mission.

Develop and maintain a unified coalition. A unified coalition provides the risk agents with their best opportunity for success. If risk agents can develop and maintain a consensus on both their proposed agenda and their revolutionary strategies, they are more likely to withstand and overcome the pressures from management. Therefore, risk leaders will need to be effective collaborators, constantly looking for and seeking a consensus among members. A unified front also makes it extremely difficult for management to divide and conquer the risk agency. Without a unified front, risk agents are vulnerable to management's counter attacks. More than anything else, a strong and unified coalition provides its members with security.

Sustaining the movement and overcoming obstacles. Risk leadership is not for the light-hearted. Risk agents must be mentally tough and willing to fight. They must be willing to risk and pay the price (whatever that might be) for doing risk leadership. To sustain important organizational change and overcome obstacles means that risk agents and their allies will need to be both stubborn and flexible. Over the long journey, they must not give up or give in if the cause is right. Yet they must learn to adapt their strategies to overcome management's attempts to stop them. Simply, risk agents must be highly committed to pursuing the revolutionary process.

Risk agents must be productive workers. During the struggle and confrontation with management, risk agents must continue to be highly effective and productive employees. They must remain an asset to their sub-unit and the organization as a whole. Again, this will provide the risk agent with real strength and security. If these revolutionaries spend most of their time on the risk leadership struggle and less time on their "actual jobs," they give management another reason to exploit and destroy the risk agency. Even beyond that, they have a responsibility to do what is right and keep the wheels of productivity moving. Risk agents must do their assigned duties and do them in a highly productive matter.

Keys to Success: Implications for Management

Willingness to accept a new shared power culture. For the organization to reach its maximum, management must be willing to accept a new organizational culture that is based, to some extent, on a shared power model. Active risk agents, for example, bring to the decision making structure new ideas and loyalty and have more ownership in the process. This new culture also means that management will need to change the way it leads the organization. Top management must be more collaborative in the way it does business. With more players at all levels involved in agenda development and implementation, the job of management will no doubt be much more difficult. However, the rewards and benefits for the organization could be tremendous.

Forgive in order to collaborate. The risk leadership model calls for risk agents and top managers to participate in a "challenge to collaborate" process where eventually the organization grows. A key step in this process involves both sides leaving conflict behind in order to reach the collaborative stage. Management (as well as risk agents, for that matter) must be willing to set aside personal feelings and forgive so all players can work together for the collective good. Management and risk agents must be willing to forgive and rebuild important relationships in order to save the organization. If these relationships are damaged beyond repair, collaboration is unlikely. The organization needs mature people at the top who have the collective interests of the company in mind.

Recognize the risk agency as a legitimate player in the organization. The sooner management accepts the legitimacy of the risk agency, the quicker real organizational progress can be made. Management must come to realize that the risk agency plays a positive role and brings value to the organization. It is important for upper management to realize the fact that risk agents and others throughout the company "have the right" to speak their minds and pursue action for the benefit of the collective good. Recognizing and legitimizing the risk agency is probably one of the most important things that management can do. Low and mid-level employees are investors and stakeholders who bring value to the decision making process. As such, they should be recognized when they help the organization.

Reward rather than punish risk taking. If management chooses to destroy the challengers, the organization loses. If management punishes risk agents, they are, in a very direct way penalizing some of the key producers of the company. These are the very people who, through their activities, have shown that they truly care about the organization and its future. A revenge strategy will only damage a risk agent's ownership, loyalty, and eventually productivity. Rewarding the risk agency also helps risk agents reintegrate into the organization following the conflict. Furthermore, rewarding positive growth is something management should be doing anyway - risk agency or not. It is important that management use its power wisely and allow for risk taking and failure among the ranks.

A partnership built on confrontation can be healthy. Some may argue that the built-in hostility approach of risk leadership will not produce the positive results desired. We disagree. Although acknowledging the dangers of risk leadership, we believe that a bipolar confrontation and competitive process can produce tremendous growth that would not otherwise be possible. We believe that the competition and the challenge of ideas are healthy for the organization. Engaging in a heated discussion over issues that are vitally important to the organization can help strengthen and support the decisions that are reached. This partnership may not always produce an efficient process, but it is likely to produce one that is best for the entire company.

Recognize the need for real change. For risk leadership to be successful, or for organizational transformation to occur, top management must at some point recognize the need for real long-term change. In most cases, convincing management may be the most difficult part of the process. Management must be willing to leave their comfortable positions and a status quo which they helped to create, to search for new and innovative solutions to organizational problems. At times they will be asked to follow the lead of risk agents who offer an alternative agenda for change. Management must be brave and not only accept change, but be advocates for it. Real change doesn't happen by accident; it must be spurred. Management must be willing to move from quick fix solutions to real transformational change.

Move to broader concerns. Like risk agents, management too must move beyond self-interest to the collective interest. If top management becomes preoccupied with consolidating power and defeating the risk agency, little progress can be made on the real issues facing the organization. Moving to the broader interest means that management must put issues of power and control aside and collaborate with others who share similar concerns. This means that at times followers must lead and leaders must follow. Management must be willing to accept a followership role while risk agents serve as "true change agents." Consensus is not an easy path, but shared leadership is one piece in putting the puzzle together. Simply, management must focus on growing the company, not just growing the profit margin.

Focus on the company's business. As with risk agents, top management too has the responsibility to focus on their duties despite the internal challenge. If management spends valuable time defending its power, the organization as a whole can lose. If management becomes so consumed by the struggle, or what they see as a win or lose situation, they will likely neglect the company's business. Important work needs to be done, and management cannot lose sight of the big picture as well as their day-to-day assignments. Successful companies have top managers who can meet the daily demands and expectations of important administrative work, while at the same time collaborate with risk leaders over the future direction of the organization.

Summary

For risk leadership to be successful and assist with the positive transformation of the organization, risk agents must be willing to lead. They must serve as collaborative change agents who represent the collective interest of the company. These brave employees must understand when to back down so they can fight another day. They need to recognize that the mobilization of the risk agency will vary from time to time and that pursuing a strategy of confrontation is a difficult balancing act. Effective risk agents must look for the right time to revolt and have a clear purpose. A successful risk agency must have broad-based involvement and support, live by a clear vision, and be able to maintain a unified front. Risk agents must pursue change that is based on reality if they hope to successfully alter the organization. They must be able to overcome the pressures and obstacles of enacting change, and their cause must serve the collective interest. Finally, risk leaders must use their power wisely and remain productive employees.

For management's part, they must be willing to legitimize the risk agency. We believe that the 21st century organization will be defined, to a great extent, by the important role low and mid-level employees play in the decision making process. Upper management must be willing to accept a new shared power culture that recognizes the risk agency as an important and legitimate organizational player. Top managers must reward rather than punish risk takers and make the difficult step toward collaboration with their subordinates. For risk leadership to succeed and the organization to improve, upper management must, above all other things, recognize the need for real and substantive change. They must also move from self-interest to supporting action that addresses broader concerns. Finally, like their counterparts, top managers must stay focused on the company's business.

Chapter 12

The Risks of Risk Leadership

Introduction

Clearly, there are risks in doing risk leadership. There are the risks of failure, the risks of job security, the risks of organizational destruction, and there are even the risks of not participating in risk leadership at all. With this chapter we will explore the risks that risk agents, top managers, and all organizational players face as they engage in this confrontational leadership approach.

The risks that risk agents face can be measured in both personal and organizational terms. As the risk agent challenges top management, they will surely risk their personal careers and job security. Top management's ability to administer punishment to subordinates is and will continue to be an issue for the revolutionaries. At the organizational level, risk agents and their risk agency risk the possibility of dividing the organization and creating a long-term hostile culture. Without careful implementation, risk leadership can, under extreme circumstances, actually destroy the organization from within. However, it is a chance we believe that needs to be taken.

While these are real concerns for those who participate in risk leadership, it should not diminish the advantages of bottom-up empowerment. By not risking risk leadership, the organization threatens its own future. Without transformational change and improvement, the organization will likely not survive anyway. Without challenging status quo thinking, the organization will probably not succeed in today's dynamic and changing business climate.

Risks for Risk Agents

First and foremost, those who choose to participate as risk agents risk the chance of failure. They risk the chance that they and the risk agency will lose the battle and possibly lose the war. The most dangerous aspect of this possibility is that the failure of a risk agency could encourage top management to reassert its power. This could mean that management would return stronger and more motivated to control the rebellious troops. Any return to a command and control management style would make all future challenges much more difficult.

On a personal level, individual risk agents and especially risk leaders risk losing organizational power and respect. They risk harming important relationships that enable them to be effective workers. Whether the risk agency succeeds or not, the revolt may damage the trust risk agents have built with many of their coworkers. It is possible, and even likely, that risk agents will be labeled as "trouble makers" in their sub-units and in the organization at large. Risk agents risk the possibility of losing valuable friends, allies, and important resources. In return, this can make it much more difficult to accomplish job-related tasks, let alone carry out the risk agency's challenge. In addition, risk agents face the real possibility of increased stress and decreased energy in their lives. At one time or another, risk agents will likely have battle fatigue.

Finally, risk agents and their allies face the real possibility of being on the blunt end of upper management's punishment efforts. When faced with power-driven managers who are more concerned about winning and less interested in the collective good, risk agents become easy targets. If the risk agency and its strategy are weak, top managers are likely to say "let's teach them a lesson" or "let's make an example of them." In extreme cases, and yet realistic ones, the risk may include job security. Since risk agents are subordinates in most cases, they do risk the possibility of damaging their careers and even facing termination. For this very reason, it is important that risk agents and their allies build a strong coalition and follow rational rather than emotional strategies. While we feel that in most situations management's tactics will likely not be that harsh, we also know and acknowledge that there are many insecure company leaders who may pursue this kind of retribution.

Risks for Management

Risk leadership also poses several risks that could impact top management's ability to effectively lead the organization. The new shared power arrangement proposed by the risk leadership model provides a series of conditions that could directly harm top management's role in producing positive organizational results. Although risk leadership calls for more players to be involved in the decision making process, it does not want to weaken upper management to the point where it can no longer effectively assist in the transformation of the organization. Remember, it is still top management that holds many of the important keys to resources and other vital components of the productivity cycle. Thus, what risk agents really want is to participate and compete with strong, capable, and effective managers who are not controlling.

The first and most obvious risk for upper management is the potential loss of power. If power is defined as the ability to influence others and events, then the loss of this ability could be harmful to the successful operation of the company. While the risk agency will likely want to keep management's power in check, it does not want to diminish that power to a point where managers cannot participate as "real change agents." This loss of organizational power could damage top managers' ability to influence key elements inside and outside the organization. For the company to be successful, it is imperative that both risk agents and upper management be strong enough to impact events.

Next, the risk leadership approach could reduce some top managers' ability to effectively make decisions. With more people involved in the leadership process of the company, it becomes much more difficult to make decisions. Often times this process can be very slow and time consuming. In today's quick moving environment, valuable opportunities could be missed. At times, the organization needs the ability to move quickly and make important decisions in the marketplace. Therefore, the risk leadership empowerment process must provide the freedom for executives to move quickly when the future of the organization is at stake.

Finally, some management types could become so fixed on the internal struggle that they risk losing focus on the important issues of productivity. It is not inconceivable to believe that many top managers will focus much of their time and energy on protecting their power and not the important issues of the day. If upper management is preoccupied with "keeping control," they risk organizational growth and improvement. Managers must keep a balance between the risk leadership processes and other important internal and external issues. The greatest risk might be that top managers will miss important opportunities. Therefore, it is imperative that executives keep at least one eye on the business landscape.

Risks for the Organization

As with risk agents and management, the organization as a whole faces its own concerns and risks. An organization led by this leadership approach is not guaranteed success. While risk leadership provides the organization with an aggressive empowerment strategy for change, it also creates an environment that could produce negative results. For example, an organization involved with internal strife can often lose sight of its mission and long-term vision. Players become so preoccupied with the issue or issues at hand, they are not able to see the bigger organizational picture. The confrontation to collaboration method proposed by risk leadership can also be time consuming. A slow decision making process can hurt the company's ability to match faster moving competitors. The polarization can also leave split loyalties and provide deep divisions and hostilities between players at all levels. As discussed earlier, the danger and results of deteriorating relationships cannot be underestimated.

Finally, the greatest risk is that the organization will crumble inward on itself. Reckless implementation of risk leadership will simply destroy the organization. Internal conflict inherent in the risk leadership process can produce conditions that, without careful monitoring, can damage the operations of the company. It would not be fair to the reader if we did not acknowledge the fact, that along with the tremendous potential of risk leadership, there is also a possibility of organizational destruction. We believe, however, that these risks are no greater than what is experienced with classical and progressive led organizations.

Risks for Not Risking

We believe that as serious as these potential risks are, *there is a greater risk in doing nothing*. While the risks encountered by risk agents, top management, and the organization in general are real and must be considered, a return to traditional methods of leadership will likely be even more dangerous for the organization. When all factors are closely examined, we believe that the advantages and results of risk leadership strategies far outweigh the potential risks for all organizational players. In fact, by doing nothing (continuing the current top-down stability and control management approaches), the organization's worst nightmares are likely to become reality. Thus, *the greater risk is in not having the will or courage to challenge the way things are done.*

The risks for not risking could have a direct threat to the survival of the organization. What is at stake is either success or failure. By not risking, we risk productivity. We risk the level of output that we produce as a collective unit. By not risking we are also accepting mediocrity and status quo thinking. We are in essence accepting an organization which says no to empowerment. By not risking we are also accepting management's claim to unfettered control. Those who do not choose to participate in risk leadership are saying no to transformation and change, and yes to stability and control. Essentially, they are accepting the failures of classical and progressive leadership.

Traditional and even more contemporary approaches to leadership have not provided the growth that many organizations need to survive. If we decide against risk leadership, against confrontational strategies, and against risking, we are accepting classical and progressive leadership. We are accepting the stability and control mandated by classical leaders and the failure of top-down empowerment and change models proposed by progressive leaders. By not risking we are allowing classical leaders to lead us in a strong hierarchical command and control style. With classical leadership, we are also accepting stability and slow incremental organizational change. By not risking we are allowing progressive leaders to dictate and control any attempt at empowerment. With progressive leadership, we are only flirting with the concepts of transformational change and improvement. Simply put, if we choose not to risk and not to implement risk leadership, we are risking the same failures experienced by those traditional managers.

Summary

Without question, there are risks in doing risk leadership. There is the risk of organizational success or failure. Risk agents face the personal risk of job termination. Top managers risk the loss of power and their ability to effectively lead the organization. On the whole, the organization even faces the risk of internal destruction. However, there are also risks for not risking risk leadership.

Those who choose to participate as risk agents face numerous challenges and threats. They risk losing against upper management, which in turn could mean stronger and more controlling leaders. Individual risk agents also risk losing organizational power and respect from those around them. Ultimately, risk agency members risk the possibility of facing punishment from their superiors.

For upper management, the risks are just as serious. They risk losing important power that enables them to play an effective role in the company's transformational efforts. By participating in risk leadership, top management also faces a much different organizational culture that could hinder decision making.

The organization as a whole also faces its own concerns and risks. For example, the risk leadership approach does not guarantee organizational success. Polarization can leave long-term divisions and hostilities within the company. Finally, the risk of risk leadership participation is that internal conflict will result in organizational destruction.

Lastly, the greatest risk of all is the risk of not risking. By not risking and endorsing risk leadership strategies, we are accepting classical and progressive leadership and the weaknesses and failures that those models represent. By not risking risk leadership, we are giving up on any chance for real empowerment.

Chapter 13

Risking Your Job is Your Job

The Risk Leadership Mandate

Risk leadership breaks away from the classical and progressive approaches to leadership and proposes a radically different model for organizational change and improvement. Risk leadership asks you to accept a completely new philosophy about how your organization should be led. It asks you to make the transition from top-down management thinking to a bottom-up confrontational approach. The risk leadership model encourages you to confront and challenge status quo authority for the purpose of transforming your organization.

Why should you confront and challenge authority? Why should you initiate confrontation at the risk of personal cost? If your organization is going to get better, it is clearly going to take more than the efforts of top management. The growth and even the survival of your organization is too important to be left in the hands of a few self-driven managers. If transformational improvement is to happen, then it is up to you and I to seize power for the good of the organization. Simply, the responsibility for the success of the organization not only rests with management, but also with low and mid-level employees who must challenge those traditional structures.

Corporate revolutionaries are bonded together by three common beliefs. First, as a risk agent, you must have a strong belief that the organization should and could be better. You see mediocrity within the system and are frustrated with what you see as little or no hope for improvement. Second, you have lost confidence in upper management's ability to successfully lead and transform your organization. To you, management does not have the desire, will, or courage to make the difficult decisions needed. Finally, you must have a deep belief that you can and should play an important role in directing and leading your company. It must be your belief that if the organization is going to grow and prosper, then it is clearly up to you.

If empowerment is to become a reality, then you and your colleagues must make it so. History shows us that classical and progressive leaders are not willing to make the personal sacrifices needed to adequately share organizational power. Therefore, if real empowerment is to be, the responsibility rests with your risk agency.

This is Your Choice - Your Future

As we see it, you have three fundamental choices. You have three futures from which to select:

Future 1. You can make the choice to continue with the status quo classical model of going to work day in and day out, being told what to do, how to do it, and where and when to do it. You can look forward to a future of security and retiring at 65 with a gold watch and a handshake. If you select this future, you are a person who prefers others to program your every move and do your thinking for you. You are letting others dictate the future of both your career and your organization. It is our belief that you should make plans for your corporate memorial, because you are on a fast track to organizational death.

Future 2. As workers under a progressive leadership model, there are certain things you can expect. First, you will be teased with the opportunity of having some control over your destiny. Progressive leaders may give you the illusion of being truly empowered, but the reality is that you will just be working for them. They still hold the cards, and they still call the plays. Second, you may see some organizational change, but it will be superficial and incremental at best. Progressive leaders often fail to test the turbulent waters of change and instead play at the shallow end of the pool. Thus, progressive led organizations are, for the most part, similar to classical led organizations which are dominated by control and stability. While your organizational death may be less painful, it is still imminent.

Future 3. Under the risk leadership approach, we avoid the fate of classical and progressive leadership. By selecting this future you have chosen an uneasy path, indeed. However, the personal and organizational rewards are too high to ignore, as are the costs of not choosing this future. Typically, organizations have been designed to create conformity, whereas risk leadership encourages workers to deviate from the norm. "Do something" is the battle cry. It is time to rally the troops. As our supervisor told us once, "I don't care what you do, just do something." Risk leadership is leadership at all levels. Risk leadership is the seizure and use of power by lower level employees. With this new power comes a responsibility to work for the collective good of the organization. Empowerment, as your guiding principle, is selfless and focused on the interests of all, rather than the interests of a few at the top. Risk leadership is not for the faint at heart, nor is it for the lazy and weak. Risk leadership is about working hard to further your organization.

What Are You Waiting For?

From the words of Reggie White of the Green Bay Packers, "It's time to fight the good fight." The time to stop talking is here. The time for action is now. It is time for action and risk leadership. It is time for you to critically look at your organization, and then look deeply inside yourself. It is time to assume responsibility.

Take a moment and stop. Yes, put this book down and eliminate all other distractions. Look out the window and answer these questions: What needs to be done? What needs improvement? What problems need to be solved? What organizations need transformed? Look at your employer, your civic groups, and even look at your child's school, and then make some decisions. Find a place to make a stand, a commitment, and a place to make a difference. Then gather the needed resources for battle.

Courageous people assume responsibility not only for themselves, but for the organizations in which they participate. They do not wait for top management, or anybody else for that matter, to provide the leadership or the authority for action. Risk leadership is a call for you to assume full and complete responsibility for the success of your company. If the organization is to grow and prosper or even survive, it is up to you and other collective-minded and passionate employees.

Personally assume responsibility for your organization and do not wait for the permission to act. If you wait, the permission will never come. Your authority comes from your willingness to act on behalf of the collective good.

You have two options: one, you can embrace and participate in risk leadership; or two, you can sit and wait for upper management to do its thing. You can be a player or a spectator. You can impact the destiny of your company, or you can watch and hope for the best. There is no question that there are risks in both options. Risk leadership brings with it danger at both the personal and organizational level. Doing nothing, however, also brings its own risks. There are no guarantees of the outcome, whether you choose risk leadership or the stability of classical and progressive leadership. However, if you select to participate in risk leadership, you have a role to play in the important decisions of the organization.

You ask - why should I? Why should I engage in such an exhausting exercise? Why should I risk my job? The answer is simple. Risk agents do it for themselves and for their organizations. Yes, do it for yourself. Be part of something that matters. Be part of something that is successful. You owe it to yourself to be an active player who impacts the company. A successful organization also means growth and opportunities for its members. Additionally, participate in risk leadership for others. Do it for your colleagues in the risk agency, for your suppliers and consumers, for top management, and do it for your community. Do it for the greater good. A successful organization provides for a healthy environment in which to live and work.

Now, look at yourself. What is it going to take? Do you have the characteristics to fight the good fight? Do you have the commitment and passion needed to carry on in the face of opposition? Do you have the ability to persist and overcome the inevitable obstacles? And are you willing to risk failure in order to succeed? If your answer is yes to these questions - what are you waiting for? It is time to assume responsibility, assess the needs of the company, build the coalition, and construct the important alternative plans for your organization. It is time to engage management by denying power, confronting, challenging, and initiating conflict when needed and when appropriate. Then it is time to look for areas of cooperation, collaboration, and ways in which a long-term partnership can be created with upper management.

Risking your job is now your job!

Bibliography

Barge, J. K. (1994). *Leadership: Communication skills for organizations and groups.* New York: St. Martin's.

Bass, B. (1985). *Leadership performance beyond expectations.* New York: The Free Press.

Bass, B. (1990). *Bass and Stogdill's handbook of leadership: Theory, research, and managerial applications.* (3rd. Ed.). New York: The Free Press.

Bennis, W. G. (1989). *On becoming a leader.* Massachusetts: Addison-Wesley Publishing Co.

Bennis, W., & Goldsmith, W. (1994). Learning to lead: A workbook on becoming a leader. Massachusetts: Addison-Wesley Publishing Co.

Bennis, W. & Nanus, B. (1985). *Leaders: The strategies for taking charge.* New York: Harper & Row.

Bolman, L. G., & Deal, T. E. (1991). *Reframing Organizations: Artistry, Choice, and Leadership.* San Francisco: Jossey-Bass Publishers.

Burns, J. M. (1978). *Leadership.* New York: Harper & Row.

Chaleff, I. (1995). The courageous follower: Standing up to and for our leaders. San Francisco: Berrett-Koehler Publishers.

Champy, J. (1995). *Reengineering management: The mandate for new leadership.* New York: HarperBusiness.

Chrislip, D. D., & Larson, C. E. (1994). *Collaborative leadership: How citizens and civic leaders can make a difference.* San Francisco: Jossey-Bass Publishers.

Clark, K. E., & Clark, M.B. (1994). *Choosing to lead.* Greensboro, NC: Leadership Press Ltd.

Clark, K. E., Clark, M. B., & Campbell, D. P.(Eds.). (1992). *Impact of leadership.* Greensboro, NC: Center for Creative Leadership.

Clark, K. E. & Clark, M. B. (Eds.), (1990). *Measures of leadership.* West Orange, NJ: Leadership Library of America, Inc.

Conger, J. (1992). *Learning to lead: The art of transforming managers into leaders.* San Francisco: Jossey-Bass Publishers.

DePree, M. (1989). *Leadership is an art.* New York: Doubleday.

Donnithorne, L. R. (Ret)(1993). *The west point way of leadership.* New York: Currency Doubleday.

Drucker, P. F. (1993). *Post-capitalist society.* New York: HarperBusiness.

Fairholm, G. W. (1993). *Organizational power politics: Tactics in organizational leadership.* Connecticut: Praeger.

Fiedler, F. E. (1967). *A theory of leadership effectiveness.* New York: McGraw-Hill.

Garderner, J. (1990). *On leadership.* New York: The Free Press.

Hughes, R. L., Ginnett, R. C., & Curphy, G. J. (1993). *Leadership: Enhancing the lessons of experience.* Homewood, IL: Irwin.

Katzenbach, J. R. (1998). *The work of teams.* Boston: Harvard Business School Press.

Kotter, J. (1990). *A force for change: How leaders differ from managers.* New York: The Free Press.

Kouzes, J. & Posner, B. (1987). *The leadership challenge: How to get extraordinary things done in organizations.* San Francisco: Jossey-Bass Publishers.

McCarthy, J. A. (1995). *The transition equation: A proven strategy for organizational change.* New York: Lexington.

McFarland, J., Senn, L. E., & Childress, J. R. (1993). *21st century leadership: Dialogues with 100 top leaders.* New York: Leadership Press.

Nadler, D. A., Shaw, R. B., Walton, A. E., & Associates (1995). *Discontinuous Change: Leading Organizational Transformation.* San Francisco: Jossey-Bass Publishers.

Northhouse, P. G. (1997). *Leadership: Theory and Practice.* California: Sage Publications, Inc.

Pfeffer, J. (1992). *Managing with power: Power and influence organizations.* Massachusetts: Harvard Business School Press.

Quinn, R. E. (1996). *Deep change: Discovering the leader within.* San Francisco: Jossey-Bass.

Rosenbach, W. E., & Taylor, R. L. (Eds.). (1993). *Contemporary issues in leadership.* Boulder, CO: Westview.

Rost, J. (1991). Leadership for the twenty-first century. New York: Praeger.

Rost, J. C. (1993). Leadership development in the new millennium. *Journal of Leadership Studies,* 1 (1), 92-110.

Schein, E. H. (1992). Organizational culture and leadership (2). San Francisco: Jossey-Bass Publishers.

Tichy, N. M. & Devanna, M. A. (1986). *The transformational leader.* New York: John Wiley & Sons.

Wren, J. T. (1995). The leader's companion: Insights on leadership through the ages. New York: The Free Press.

Yukl, G. A. (1989). *Leadership in organizations.* Englewood Cliffs, NJ: Prentice-Hall.